Reality, Knowledge, and Value

Reality, Knowledge, and Value

A BASIC INTRODUCTION

TO PHILOSOPHY

Jerome A. Shaffer, UNIVERSITY OF CONNECTICUT

RANDOM HOUSE, NEW YORK

TO MY PARENTS

PREFACE

The purpose of this book is to introduce the reader to some of the basic problems of philosophy—particularly, problems in the fields of metaphysics, epistemology, and ethics. No prior formal training in philosophy is needed in order to understand any part of the book. In this respect, it is a book for beginners in philosophy. Yet it is a peculiarity of philosophy that it is a short step from the posing of many of the questions it raises to the very frontiers of human knowledge. Thus, in many cases the reader is carried to the point at which the most recent scholarly work is being done. He may progress in a twinkling from novice to advanced thinker. This is one feature of philosophy that makes it so exciting.

Another exciting feature of philosophy is that its problems are the basic intellectual problems of mankind—the problems that any rational person ought to consider. What exists? What can be known? What is important? This book, I hope, will encourage and help the reader to come to some conclusions for himself. Sometimes I make reference to the views of historical figures; I do this not so much to provide information about these philosophers as to indicate the age-old and perennial nature of the problems. Sometimes I indicate my own conclusions; I do this not because I believe they have much lasting importance, but because I would like to give the reader the idea that the point of philosophy is not to learn everyone else's opinions but to arrive at one's own.

I would like to acknowledge some of the help I have received in writing this book. I was introduced to these problems and convinced of their importance by the late Arthur E. Murphy at Cornell; I hope that he would approve of the spirit in which this is written. William K. Frankena, Joel J. Kupperman, and Maxwell F. Littwin made useful suggestions concerning the manuscript. It was begun while I was a Fellow at the Center for Advanced Study in the Behavioral Sciences in Stanford; I appreciate the countless aids I received from that magnificent institution (and hope it will fully recover from its recent fire-bombing), and I wish especially to mention the wonderful secretarial help of Mrs. Anna C. Tower. I have profited a good deal from discussions of most of the topics in this book with my colleagues Garry M. Brodsky, Keith E. Halbasch, A. S. McGrade, and Samuel Wheeler. I have found invaluable the comments and encouragement of my warm friends, Monroe and Elizabeth Beardsley, and of my wife, Olivia. I look forward to the reactions of Diana and David, when they learn to read.

JEROME A. SHAFFER

Storrs, Connecticut
August 13, 1970

CONTENTS

Reality, Knowledge, and Value

1

Plato's Parable of the Cave

Over 2,000 years ago the Greek philosopher Plato formulated one of the basic problems of philosophy in a striking
image. He asked us to imagine an underground cave with its
entrance open toward the light. Inside this cave, facing the
wall, are prisoners who, from childhood onward, have had
chains on their legs and necks preventing them from leaving
the cave or even moving their heads. All they can see is a
wall on which are cast shadows of objects behind them—
shadows of men, animals, and machines. Such people would
have no idea of the real objects that were casting the shadows
or of the ways in which the shadows were produced. This
world of shadow objects would be the only world they would
know, and they would take it to be the only world there was.
If, said Plato, one of their members were to escape and go out

into the sunlight and then come back and try to tell the captives in the cave about the outside world, the captives would think him insane and filled with visions; certainly they would not believe him.

How do we know, asked Plato, that we are not in a position very similar to the captive people of this story? How do we know that the world around us is not a shadow world too, and that the real world, which is unknown to us, is utterly different?

Common sense tells us that the world is essentially the way it appears to be. It tells us that there are a number of physical objects like tables, chairs, trees, and human bodies that have existed, do now exist, and will continue to exist in the future very much the way they seem to. Common sense tells us that some of these material objects—those we call human beings—are conscious beings who think and wonder and have feelings and hopes and are self-consciously *aware* that they have these thoughts and feelings. Science adds to this commonsense picture the doctrines that these material objects and that special group of them that we call human beings, on the one hand, are composed of billions and billions of very small bits of matter-energy, and, on the other hand, are themselves only one small part of a much larger object called the Earth, which is itself a relatively small body surrounded by billions and billions of other bodies that make up the universe. This composite picture of science and commonsense is one that all of us, more or less, accept.

How do we know that this world view is correct? Perhaps we and our whole universe are just one molecule in some fantastically larger object—perhaps a worm. Perhaps that worm is itself just one speck of some yet larger universe. Perhaps, as in the case of the captives of Plato's myth, the world we see is some crude and inaccurate distortion of a world that in its own nature is very different. Do the appearances with which we are so familiar in our daily lives and in our scientific investigations represent in any accurate way the fundamental nature of things? And even if they do, have we any reason to believe that this is the case? All we can know is the appearance presented to us, and so we can never tell how close it comes to the reality behind.

We have just raised the fundamental questions of *metaphysics* and *epistemology*. Metaphysics is the branch of philosophy that is concerned with trying to discern the fundamental nature of reality as it really is, as opposed to as it appears to bè. It asks such questions as: Is the physical world the only world? Does the mind really exist? What is the relationship between them? Is everything in the world totally determined by the laws of nature? Does man have free will? Is there a God? Is there an afterlife? Epistemology (literally, the theory of knowledge) is the branch of philosophy that is concerned with questions of what can and cannot be known. It is concerned with such questions as: Can anything be known for certain, or is probability the best that we can ever get? Are there some areas in which we can get higher probabilities than in others? How can we know about the past, since it no longer exists? How can we know about the future, when it has not happened yet? Can we trust our senses to give us reliable knowledge about the world? Are there other ways of knowing than by using our senses?

In our everyday life, we do not raise these questions. We assume that things are essentially the way they seem to be and that by observing how things seem to be, we can determine fairly accurately how things really are. This goes not only for the housewife in her kitchen, but also for the scientist in his laboratory. These people investigate and test hypotheses all the time, but they assume the basically commonsense point of view. It is the task of philosophy to look more deeply into some of these matters and to try to determine whether the assumptions of the commonsense-scientific viewpoint are defensible. The important and disturbing point of Plato's parable of the cave is that it is *possible* that our assumptions are not valid for reality or at best are only valid for that tiny portion of reality that we happen to observe. Once we recognize that it is possible, it becomes an interesting question whether or not we are, in fact, in a position like that of Plato's captives.

2

How Do I Know I Am
Not Now Dreaming?

Let us start our investigation into metaphysics and epistemology by raising a specific question: How do I know I am not now dreaming? This question was posed by Plato and, later, by the father of modern philosophy, Descartes, who published his *Meditations on First Philosophy* in 1641. How do I know I am not now dreaming? Well, everything certainly *seems* perfectly normal. The book that I am looking at now *seems* clear and sharp to me. The room I am in *seems* perfectly normal and real. There is nothing particularly strange or unusual going on right now. It certainly *seems* that I am wide awake. But still we must remember that people frequently have very realistic *dreams*—dreams in which everything *seems* to be quite normal. If dreams didn't seem so real to us, then things that happen in dreams would never frighten us. But as we know, we sometimes get quite frightened by a dream because it does seem to be so real. Perhaps I am at this very minute in bed having a most realistic dream, dreaming that I am sitting at my desk, reading a philosophy book. It is certainly possible that there might be a dream just like this. How do I know that *this* is not such a dream?

If I seriously raised the question, How do I know I am not now dreaming?—I might feel that there are things I could do to determine whether it is a dream or not. For example, I could try pinching myself, slapping myself in the face, getting up and stretching, or reciting "Abou Ben Adhem." Yet what would this show? For is it not quite possible that I should *dream* that I am pinching myself, slapping my face, getting up and stretching, or reciting "Abou Ben Adhem"? One can imagine that kind of dream occurring. How do I know that this is not that kind of dream? Suppose I try to do a little experiment. I seem to remember writing my name in the front of this book, and I predict that it will still be there. So, if I look in the front of the book and find it there, this will confirm my seeming to remember that I did write it there, and perhaps that will show that I am now awake. But suppose I look and I see my name in the front of the book. What does this show? Surely I can dream that I put my name there, surely I can dream that I am now checking, and surely I can dream that I am now finding my name there. We have still not broken out of the dream world. Suppose I try to remember something difficult—the names of all the states, for example. Can I not also dream that I am remembering them? Suppose that I try doing a mathematical problem in my head. Can I not dream that I am trying to do a mathematical problem in my head? Can I not dream that I have solved it successfully? It does not seem that any test that I try to perform will prove anything, because I can never be sure whether I am actually performing the test or merely dreaming that I am performing it; and I can never be sure whether the outcome of the test is successful or whether I am only dreaming that the outcome of the test is successful. So, in general, it looks as though there is no way of showing that I am now awake and not dreaming.

The following thought may occur to you: I grant that I cannot be *sure*, cannot *prove* that I am now awake, but I can at least make it *probable* that I am awake. But this thought would miss the fundamental point of our problem. It is not that I cannot *prove* that I am awake; it is that there does not seem to be even *the slightest reason* for thinking that I am now awake. All of the apparent evidence that I have—the way things appear to be now—have no weight at all if I am only dreaming them. No matter how much like waking life all of this seems to me to be, the fact remains that I may well be dreaming that everything is going on normally. So the fact that everything seems to be going on normally gives not the slightest weight to the supposition that I am awake. For all I know, this may be a very realistic dream, and I cannot infer from the realistic appearances that it is *not* a realistic dream.

"Well," you might say, "what does it matter? If it is a very realistic dream, then that is just the same as being awake, so who cares whether it is a dream or waking life?" But it obviously does matter. If this is all a dream, then, for example, you are not awake and studying now, so that you are not getting your philosophy assignment done. You may find yourself waking up in the next few minutes to discover that you have overslept and missed your class. Here the importance of deciding whether it is a dream or not is based on the importance of having some reasonable expectations about what is going to happen next. Of course, it is true that even if this is a dream, it is a pleasant enough dream—let us hope even an interesting dream. But suppose that in the next few minutes things begin to get more unpleasant. Suppose your roommate rushes in with some bad news. Suppose you suddenly notice a person creeping toward you with a knife. Then it will be quite important whether it is a dream or not—whether you are really in danger or not. Of course, we can't go through our lives constantly asking ourselves, Is this a dream or not? But this does not mean that we should *never* raise the question. Here is one comparatively convenient time to raise this question, and we have seen that once it is raised, it does not seem very easy to answer.

The problem we have been discussing so far is a problem in epistemology. That is to say, it is a problem concerned with what can be known and how it is to be known, if it can be known. We can see connected with this epistemological problem a metaphysical problem, that is, a problem concerned with the nature of reality. The metaphysical problem would be this: How are the things that happen in dreams different in their basic nature from the things that happen in "real life"? We have already seen that the difference cannot lie in whether what happens is normal or ordinary or "realistic," since dreams may be exactly like real life in their content. In fact, that is what makes us believe during the dream that these things are really happening. So the difference between dreams and real life cannot be in the content of each. It must be something else. But what is the difference, then, between something that happens in a dream and something that happens in real life? Might the difference consist only in this: What we call "real life" is simply an elaborate, consistent, prolonged dream; and what we call "a dream" is a comparatively short sequence that does not fit in with the longer part? Here is another possibility. Perhaps each person in the world is having his own dream, but all the dreams are in phase, so that when you dream you are speaking with your roommate, he at the same time is dreaming that he is speaking with you. Here would be a case where there was a common world to some degree, although each of us existed only in his dream world.

There are a number of different possibilities here. All of these would be somewhat different metaphysical schemes. Each would give us a somewhat different account of the ultimate nature of things. We see how intertwined epistemology and metaphysics are when we notice that each of these metaphysical schemes is possible and that the epistemological question of whether we have any reason for believing that our world is one way rather than another is always pertinent.

3

Can Anything Be Known?

If you have no reason for thinking that you are now awake, then you have no reason for thinking that your present situation is actually what it seems to be. For all you know, you might be at this moment back in bed, sound asleep. But not only are all of your beliefs about your present situation cast in doubt; all of your beliefs about the whole world and your place in it are also cast in doubt. For example, you believe that the earth is round. But this belief is based upon what you seem to remember and seem to know about the laws of nature. All of these might be in error, for it is quite possible that you might wake up and say, "I just had a curious dream; I dreamed the earth was round." How about your beliefs about your own past—for example, that you went to a particular high school? Here again, this might all be a part of your dream. You might be dreaming that you were born in a particular place, that you graduated from a particular high school, and so on. Once we admit the possibility that we are now dreaming, all of our beliefs about the world become a part of that dream, and to that extent, they become infected with doubt. "But," you might say, "how about the belief that people sometimes dream? Isn't that a belief that we must keep if we are to raise these doubts?" No, even that may be doubtful. All we need for our doubts is the *possibility* that this might be a dream. As soon as we admit that it is a possibility, then we see that all of our beliefs are doubtful if we cannot eliminate that possibility.

How about abstract truths—the truths of logic and mathematics, for example? Even these are to some degree doubtful. Consider the Pythagorean Theorem. Perhaps you are only dreaming that that is true. "Well," you might say, "I can prove it." But how do you know you are really proving it, as opposed to simply dreaming that you are proving it? Could one not dream that he had proved some statement, only to wake up and see that the proof was fallacious? How about arithmetic truths? Here, too, error is possible. Don't people sometimes misremember 11×12 or even $8 + 5$? So, *in principle at least,* it is possible to get something as simple as $2 + 2$ wrong. It seems as though nothing is safe from doubt once we have raised the possibility of dreaming. We are, at this point, in very much the same place as Descartes found himself. What did he do? Descartes tried to carry his doubts to their ultimate conclusion. He tried to be skeptical of *his own existence.* He said, "Perhaps I do not exist either. But," he continued, "I think that I exist. So, if I do not exist, then I am dreaming that I exist, or in some other way am deceived into thinking that I exist." And then Descartes noticed a very simple, very obvious, but very important truth. He noticed that in order to dream that he exists or otherwise be deceived into thinking that he exists—in other words, in order to *think* that he exists, *he must exist.* "*Cogito ergo sum* (I think therefore I am). Even if the existence of all else is in doubt, my own existence cannot be doubted by me." And so here we have a very simple but apparently unshakable argument that each one of us can produce to prove his own existence to himself.

Let us see how Descartes continued from this slender beginning. Having proved that "I exist" can be known to be true as soon as it is thought, Descartes then went on to ask what this "I" is. He argued that since the body that one seems to have might be imaginary or some sort of deception, this "I" cannot be a body. It must be simply a thing that thinks—that is, a thing that wonders, doubts, imagines, and so forth. Descartes then noted that one of the ideas that this "I" has is the idea of God, and from the existence of this idea, Descartes tried to prove the existence of God. Having proved, at least to his own satisfaction, that God exists, he then asserted that God is necessarily good. If God allows me to have all these beliefs about the world—past, present, and future—and yet it is still the case that all these beliefs are in error, then, said Descartes, God would be a deceitful being, and therefore not good. Since God is good, and therefore cannot be a deceitful being, it may be concluded that we cannot always be in error about the world but must, at least for the most part, be correct in our beliefs about it. Therefore, he argued, the complete skepticism that we seem to have fallen into is not justified. We can know at least this much—that if we think about things for a long time, it is likely that we will come to the truth about things. The alternative to this would be that God is a deceitful being, something that, by nature of his goodness, He cannot be. So here we see how Descartes tries to get us out of the general skepticism we seem to have fallen into. Specifically, so far as the problem of dreams is concerned, if we try to carry out the various tests such as pinching or slapping ourselves, reciting "Abou Ben Adhem," and other experiments for a time and things go on as if we were awake, then it becomes reasonable to think we are awake. What makes it reasonable is that we were created by a good God who does not wish us to be constantly in error.

Descartes' system has been presented as an epistemological system, that is, as an answer to the question, What can be known? It also contains a metaphysical aspect. Descartes' metaphysics is as follows: The basic reality is a divine, all-powerful, all-knowing, all-good God. There also exist, through God's creation and constant preservation, other sorts of entities. These fall into two classes. There are the physical substances, that is, *matter,* the essential characteristic of which is that it occupies space. Then there are also thinking things, that is, *selves,* the essence of which is to be capable of various kinds of mental activity. In certain cases, these two kinds of substances are in close interaction. A human being is a case of the union of a thinking thing and a corporeal (material) thing. Both components are so closely interdependent one upon the other that they form a single unified system.

Descartes' system is one of the great achievements in man's intellectual history. It is a masterpiece of philosophical inquiry, both for the problems it raises and for the ingenious attempts to solve them. Nevertheless, there have been many important criticisms of Descartes' solution over the years, and much of his solution would be rejected by the consensus of philosophic thinkers today. The greatness of Descartes' system lies in his awareness of the major problems of epistemology and metaphysics and in the attempt to meet these problems in a consistent, coherent, justifiable way.

In the following sections of this book, we shall examine in more detail some of the major problems of philosophy. We shall discuss whether anything at all can be known for certain (sections 4 through 6); what we can know of the material world and what, in very general terms, its nature is (sections 7 through 10); and the nature of the self and its relation to the human body (sections 11 through 14). We shall conclude with a discussion of value and the meaning of life. Although these are only a few of the questions in the fields of epistemology, metaphysics, and ethics, they are typical of these fields and among the most important questions. In some places we shall try to come to tentative conclusions. In others we shall be content merely to indicate the most telling considerations on each side and let the reader attempt to reach his own conclusions.

4

The Problem of Certainty—
The Fallibilist Position

Descartes, as we have seen, argued that our beliefs about the world are not *certain*, because, for all we know, we may simply be dreaming that the world is the way it seems to us to be. Now of course we could be dreaming these things and our beliefs might still be true. For example, I might dream that during the night a person came into my room, and, as a matter of fact, at that moment a person might actually have come into my room. What the arguments based upon the possibility of dreaming show, if anything, is not merely that our beliefs about the world might be false, but, more important, that our beliefs about the world are *unwarranted* and *unjustified*. The use of the notion of dreaming serves as a dramatic way of reminding us that we could be perceiving all the appearances we are perceiving and it might still be the case that things are not really the way the appearances indicate that they are. For purposes of raising doubts, we might have pointed out not that we might be dreaming, but, for example, that we might be temporarily insane and locked up in some little padded cell having the psychotic hallucination that we are studying philosophy, with the doctors peering in through the little peephole, shaking their heads sadly and saying, "Poor chap, he still thinks he is studying philosophy." Or we might be at present terribly drunk, under hypnosis, drugged, or in some other abnormal state.

We can characterize this situation more clearly by distinguishing between a person's *feeling certain* that, for example, Hitler is dead and its *being certain* that Hitler is dead. The first is a psychological state—a feeling of utter confidence and lack of the slightest hesitancy; most of us have such feelings about a number of things. On the other hand, the second is about the actual grounds, evidence, or support for the assertion that Hitler is dead. If it is certain, then the grounds for the assertion must be overwhelming and complete. From the fact that we feel certain it does not follow that it is certain, that is, that our feeling of certainty is justified. Now we often do feel certain about our beliefs about the world, but the possibility of dreams is meant to show us that we may not be *justified* in feeling certain.

Let us use the term "fallibilist" to mean someone who holds, concerning some particular group of beliefs, that we are never justified in feeling certain about any of them. We must now consider some of the fallibilist arguments.

One argument is traditionally called "the argument from illusion," but it might be better to call it "the argument from the possibility of deception." It starts by pointing out the possibility of dreams, insanity, hallucination, and so forth. Now what do these possibilities indicate? They indicate that there is a distinction to be made between how things are at a particular time and how things seem to be at that time. We can imagine or conceive of situations in which things might seem to be one way and, because it is all a dream, things might actually be quite different. So no matter how much evidence we get, it still bears on the appearances and not on the reality. So we must remain forever in doubt about the reality.

Another argument might be called "the argument from the incompleteness of the evidence." When we talk about how things seem to us, we are always referring to the appearances up to some particular time, that is, how things appear to us *now*. But there is still the future to take into account. That things now seem to us one way does not rule out the possibility that the nature of the evidence will begin to change and things will begin to look quite different to us. Something like this happens in the case of dreaming. I may now seem to be reading a philosophy book, but in the next minute and from then onward it may seem to me that I had merely been dreaming that I was reading a philosophy book, since I may suddenly find myself in my bed and things may go on from there in such a way as to make it seem as though this had all been a dream. So in order to know how things are, I must not only know how things seem to me now, but also how things will continue to seem to me in the future. Since the future is still to come, and since no matter how much time passes there will still be more future to come, I can never be certain how things are. The evidence is always incomplete.

The argument from the incompleteness of the evidence is more worrisome than the argument from the possibility of deception. The latter argument simply reminds us that no matter how much evidence we get, we are still faced with the (bare) possibility that we are mistaken. The former shows that no matter how much evidence we have, we could begin to get *counterevidence* that would actually show us we were mistaken all along, so it represents a more threatening situation.

How far is fallibilism warranted? Does it apply to what philosophers have called "a priori propositions"? Some examples of such propositions would be, "All bachelors are males," "Things equal to the same thing are equal to each other," and "The cube root of 216 is 6." A defining mark of such propositions is that they need not be established as true by appealing to experience, for example, by inspecting thousands of bachelors. Many fallibilists would not wish to claim that such propositions were uncertain. However, Descartes himself felt that such propositions were open to doubt (at least so long as the existence of a good God had not been proved). The two fallibilist arguments we have just used could well be applied in such cases to show that these propositions were not certain. Even in these cases the best that we could show at any particular time would be that such propositions appeared to us to be incontrovertibly true—not that they really were. Also, is it not always possible that in the next instance we might suddenly notice a flaw in our reasoning or an error in our judgment that would reduce our confidence in the proposition? For example, is it not possible that one should dream that $3 + 2 = 7$ and during the dream feel absolutely certain that this is a mathematical truth? Only on awakening might one see the error. So there is no reason why fallibilism, as we have sketched it here, must apply only to truths about the world known through sense experience. Fallibilism applies just as much to a priori truths.

Does fallibilism apply also to statements about how things seem to me right now? Descartes thought not. He said that even if I think I see light or hear noise or feel heat but do not really see these things because I am in a state of hallucination, "still it is at least quite certain that it seems to me that I see light, that I hear noise, and that I feel heat" (second *Meditation*). Even if I am mistaken in thinking I am perceiving how things are, it is certain that it seems to me that I am perceiving things the way they are.

Can fallibilism be applied to these seems-to-me-now statements? Are they also not quite certain? Can they not also be subject to some real doubt? This much seems clear. The two reasons for doubt that apply to statements about how things are—namely, that there might be a discrepancy between how things seem to me now and (1) how they really are now or (2) how things will seem to me later on—do not apply here. For example, suppose I am having an hallucination in which

I seem to see a dagger before me (remember Macbeth). Now in this situation, if I say, "There is a dagger here before me," then I will be saying something that is false, and I will be mistaken. If other experience, for example, no one else's seeing the dagger or finding any traces of it, or my own later failure to see it, should occur, then I may have to admit that I was mistaken in my belief that there was a dagger there. And, within the fallibilist frame of reference, since it is always possible that such new experiences will occur, we can never be certain about any statement about how things are. However, suppose I make the more cautious, guarded claim not that there is a dagger there, but merely that there now seems to me to be a dagger there. Then, later observations may show that there is no dagger there, but they will not show that I was wrong when I said, *"It now seems to me* that there is a dagger here." In fact, no future discoveries about how things are or seem later on could overthrow my claim that *at that moment* they *seemed* a particular way to me.

The statements we have been considering—statements in which I report how things seem to me—are special examples of a large variety of statements that people make about their own present conscious states. I shall call such statements "introspective reports." Reports of sensations are examples of introspective reports. Consider the statement "I have a headache." Such a statement reports the occurrence of a particular event—a headache. Now suppose that doctors investigate very carefully the state of my body, and discover that there is no organic cause for this headache. This would not cast any doubt on the truth of my report that I have a headache. It would make no sense for anyone to say that investigations showed that I didn't have a headache but only *thought* I had a headache. There is no such thing as being deceived about headaches in the sense that one seems to have a headache but in fact doesn't. Seeming to have a headache and having a headache are one and the same thing. Let us take another sort of report of inner experience—the report of a thought. Suppose I say, "It just occurred to me that it is time to go to the train." Could I *think* I had just had this thought and be mistaken? To have the thought, to think the thought, and to think I thought the thought are all one and the same thing. We shall have more to say about introspective reports later on (see section 11), but for now what is important to notice is that the kinds of doubts that arise concerning a possible discrepancy between how things seem to me and how things are do not apply here.

It is desirable to distinguish these introspective reports from reports that include an introspective element but contain a nonintrospective element as well. If I say, "I have a pain in my little toe," I report a pain but also ascribe to it a physical location in my body. Here a new opportunity for error arises, for it may be shown that the pain is not in my little toe but in the next one. It may even turn out that, unbeknownst to me, my foot has been amputated and it merely seems to me that I have a pain in my little toe. Many sensation reports are mixed; even "toothache," "headache," and so forth, can be interpreted as ascribing a physical location. But it is always possible to frame judgments that have no nonintrospective element—for example, I have a pain that seems to be in a tooth—and it is these judgments we have in mind when we talk of "introspective reports."

Now let us turn back to the question of whether such reports as these, that is, introspective reports, are fallible. That is to say, is it possible that a person should make such reports and be mistaken? Consider reports of *past* conscious states. Could I say that I had a headache yesterday morning, and be mistaken about that? Yes, of course. Here my memory may play tricks upon me and I may make a mistake. The best I can do is to say that it now seems to me that I had a headache yesterday morning or that I now seem to remember that I had a headache yesterday morning. What we are concerned with here are present-tense reports, or reports concerning the immediate past, which is accessible without exercising memory, as in the report, "Just now I had the feeling that . . ." If I say, "I have a headache now," does this mean that *you*

cannot doubt my statement, or that what I am saying cannot
be false? No, of course not, because I may be lying, for example. So what is important here is that the statement be a sincere statement. And it must be about *myself*. Suppose I say,
"*He* has a headache now." This clearly does not come under
our heading of introspective reports, since it is not about myself but about another person. Such a statement is open to all
of the doubts that statements about the world are open to,
and perhaps more.

Well now, if I make a sincere first-person, present-tense report, then can what I say be false? Yes, there still is an important loophole open. Suppose I am not very well acquainted
with the language, or, in making my report, make some slip
of the tongue. Suppose I say, "I have a toothache," when what
I meant to say was, "I have a headache." Here what I say will
be wrong because of a verbal error. So if we are going to consider the case for infallibility in this area, we must confine
ourselves not to actual reports that may be insincere or contain verbal errors, but to the *judgments* or *beliefs* that we
have and to which we give expression when we make reports.
Can such introspective judgments or beliefs be mistaken?
Many philosophers have thought that here we reach a bedrock
of certainty, a set of judgments that could not possibly be
false.

But even here mistakes are possible. Mistakes are possible
because, even when our task is only to identify the experience,
it is possible that we might come up with the wrong identification. You shut your eyes and we give you a spoonful of ice
cream. Isn't it possible that you might first say it tasted like
peach to you and then take it back and become quite sure it
tasted like strawberry? Here your mistake was that of not making the correct identification, not attaching the correct label.
Some people are better than others at discriminating flavors,
and a person might, over time, improve. This does not mean
necessarily that the character of his experience changes (although that may happen too). It may mean that he becomes
better at identifying with precision the nature of his experi-

ence. The same thing goes for people who are able to distinguish different colors or shades of color. Here we have errors that come about through lack of practice in making these discriminations and therefore lack of skill in making them. It is unlikely in many of these cases that the person does not know the meanings of such expressions as, "It tastes to me like peach ice cream" or, "It tastes to me like strawberry ice cream." These are errors that arise through lack of expertise in making the proper identifications. Other sources of error are lack of attention and carelessness in making judgments. Is it not possible that it may seem to me to be a headache but then, after attention and care, turn out to be a toothache instead? So error does seem possible even here.

But surely, one feels like saying, in perfectly obvious cases no mistake is possible. If a man suffers a severe burn, surely he will be in intense pain, and in these circumstances could he possibly be mistaken in his judgment as to whether he was in pain or not? Even here, the fallibilist would claim that we are forced to admit that error might occur. For example, consider a religious martyr being burned at the stake. Is it not possible that he should be concentrating so completely on his religious experiences that he might not really be aware of the pain itself? If a sadistic bystander asked him whether he was in pain or not, the martyr might, mistakenly, say he was not in pain and then realize after shifting his attention that he was in pain. And might there not also be cases where the martyr might say without thinking that he was in pain and then notice to his surprise that he was not in pain? So the best we can say, according to the fallibist, is that in such cases error is fantastically unlikely, but still possible. (The antifallibist might say that the martyr was so carried away by his religious ecstasy that he ceased to be in pain.)

Finally let us return to Descartes' *"Cogito ergo sum."* Here, Descartes argued, certainly can be found. But could not a persistent fallibilist make trouble for Descartes even here? First of all, how do I know that I think? Perhaps it is not thinking but something else. Still, Descartes would say, I think that I think, or, in other words, it seems to me that I think. But now we are back with seems-to-me statements, and we have seen that these are open to skeptical doubts. Furthermore what is this *I* that thinks? Is it some kind of entity that lasts over time? Have I ever observed this I? Can I say without doubt that this I exists? As many philosophers have pointed out, what one should say instead of "I think" is "there is a thought now," and then we must *infer* from the occurrence of this thought to the existence of a thinker. Furthermore, the original *"Cogito ergo sum"* seems to be an inference from "I think" to "I am." So here we have double inference, from the existence of the thought to the existence of the thinker to the existence of the "I" or self. And, as Descartes himself pointed out, wherever there is inference, there is the possibility of mistaken inference, even when the inference is quite simple. So "I think therefore I am" does seem to be open to a number of fallibilist objections.

Let us go to an even more basic formulation. At one point Descartes expressed the basic proposition in the following way: "I exist" is necessarily true each time that I pronounce it or mentally conceive it. This leads to the claim that a person's belief in his own existence must be a true belief. It is, of course, easy to see why this must be the case. A person must exist in order to believe something; if a person believes something he must exist in order to believe it. And this applies whether he believes it correctly or mistakenly. So if a person exists, then his belief that he exists will be true. But none of this tells us whether any person does exist. All of these hypothetical statements might be true without anyone's existing at all. In order for me to know that I exist I must know that I believe in my existence. If I believe in my existence, then I do exist, and my belief is true. But how do I know that I do believe in my existence? That is to say, how do I know that a person exists who believes in his own existence? Well, at least it seems to me that I exist and believe in my own existence. But now we are back to the earlier formulation, "I think therefore I am," and we have already seen the difficulties there.

5

The Problem of Certainty—The Reply to the Fallibilist

If the fallibilist is right in his thinking, then no statement can be known with certainty. All our beliefs are to some degree doubtful. Some statements are a little bit more secure, in that they are not open to certain kinds of doubts, but in all cases error is possible. Let us hope that the fallibilist has the humility to admit that even his own claim that no statement is certain is itself to some degree doubtful (he is in trouble if he refuses to admit that).

The claim that every statement is to some degree doubtful has often seemed ludicrous to ordinary men and to some philosophers in their ordinary moments. Even Descartes had his reservations about his own fallibilism and said of such beliefs as "there is in truth a world" and "men possess bodies" that these were beliefs "which never have been doubted by anyone of sense" (in his synopsis of the *Meditations*). If we found a man who actually had some doubts about whether he had a body, would we not advise him to go to a psychiatrist? If a man who had just caught his finger in a door said, "Well, I believe I am in considerable pain, but I admit it is not certain that I am," would we not think that the pain had somehow affected his mind, that he was somehow in shock, or the like? If a person actually had some reservations about asserting that $3 + 4 = 7$, we would not applaud him for his caution but chide him for his ignorance of mathematics.

There is, then, among reasonable men, a natural inclination to agree in certain circumstances that particular judgments are known for certain. If we have any grasp of the meaning of "certain," we should think that such cases as those above are perfectly good cases for using that term. If this is a mistake, and no statement is ever certain, then a very powerful argument must be provided to show this. We had better look again at the fallibilist approach.

The general way in which the fallibilist attempted to show that no statement is ever certain was by pointing out that in each case an error was *possible,* in the sense that a person could imagine circumstances that would lead him to believe a proposition that was false. But why would this show that every belief is to some degree doubtful or uncertain? I do not cast doubt upon a person's report by showing that *if* he had been drunk at the time, his report would have been worthy of doubt. I do not cast doubt upon a person's report by showing that *if* he had been inattentive, his report would have been worthy of doubt. I cast doubt upon a person's report only if I can provide some reason for thinking he *was* drunk or inattentive or the like at the time. If there is no reason to think that the person was drunk or inattentive at the time and good reason to think he was sober and attentive, then we are not entitled to have reservations about the truth of his report simply because of the bare possibility that he might have been drunk or inattentive at the time. The fallibilist seems to make the illegitimate move from "If he was drunk, his report is not certain" to "His report is not certain."

What do we mean when we say of a particular statement that it is certain? I would suggest that what we mean is that we could not become more justified than we now are in believing it. When I say that it is certain that $2 + 2 = 4$, I imply that we would not be more justified in believing it if we asked some eminent mathematician whether it is true or did the sum once more. When I say that it is certain that I am now in pain, what I mean is that it would be pointless for me to pay particular attention to my state in order to increase my confidence in my belief that I am in pain. On this interpretation of "certain" the antifallibilist claims that in some cases we reach a point where no further support need be sought for a particular belief. The fallibilist believes that we never reach such a point. Who is right? At this point it does seem to be the case that the antifallibilist is right, since, to take our examples again, it would be ludicrous for a man to think that he could become more and more justified in believing the proposition "$2 + 2 = 4$" or the proposition "I am in pain" if he continued to test it again and again.

The fallibilist might grant that it becomes pointless to try to seek out new confirming evidence for our beliefs in some cases, but he might still hold that these beliefs are open to doubt. He might argue as follows, using the argument from the possibility of deception: For any belief we can imagine some subsequent events that ought to shake our confidence in those beliefs. Therefore the fact that such things do *not* happen should *increase* our confidence in those beliefs. For example, our confidence that $2 + 2 = 4$ should continue to increase as time passes and still no eminent mathematician contradicts our belief. Although the degree of confidence we are justified in having would continue to increase, there would never be a point at which further increase was impossible; that is to say, there would never be a point at which we reached certainty. We would get closer and closer to certainty but never reach it.

The antifallibilist claims that there comes a point when we do reach certainty. When we have reached this point, we do not have to wait with our hearts in our mouths, hoping that no new upsetting information will arrive. To return to our example, $2 + 2 = 4$, we know perfectly well, know for certain, that no mathematician will upset the truth of this arithmetic proposition. Our confidence should not increase as time passes and no such mathematician steps forward. Our confidence could not increase. We have maximum confidence in this proposition. In the case of "I am now in considerable pain," we reach this stage very quickly. A person need only reflect for a moment and he will have achieved the state where maximum confidence is warranted. In the case of "I have a body," perhaps a little longer period is needed before we will say it is certain. But we reach this stage without difficulty also. The possibility of error in such cases is admitted, but a mere possibility is absolutely no reason to think that there is some justifiable doubt with respect to the truth of the statement.

We seem to have reached an impasse in our discussion of fallibilism. The fallibilist claims that the mere *possibility* that there might be counterevidence should lead us to have less than complete confidence. His opponent holds that it is not enough to point out the mere possibility of counterevidence; one must get some of this counterevidence before confidence should be diminished. It is very difficult to see which one of these sides is correct. This happens frequently in philosophy. We are torn between two viewpoints, each persuasively argued, and it is impossible to say which of these is correct. We find ourselves first pushed one way and then the other. We seem to find ourselves in such a dilemma here. What are we to do?

6

The Problem of Certainty—
Two Kinds of Certainty?

A solution that is favored by many philosophers today is suggested by a device used from the very beginning of philosophy itself—the making of a distinction. The following anecdote by the pragmatist philosopher William James illustrates this device:

> Some years ago, being with a camping party in the mountains, I returned from a solitary ramble to find every one engaged in a ferocious metaphysical dispute. The *corpus* of the dispute was a squirrel—a live squirrel supposed to be clinging to one side of a tree-trunk; while over against the tree's opposite side a human being was imagined to stand. This human witness tries to get sight of the squirrel by moving rapidly round the tree, but no matter how fast he goes, the squirrel moves as fast in the opposite direction, and always keeps the tree between himself and the man, so that never a glimpse of him is caught. The resultant metaphysical problem now is

this: *Does the man go round the squirrel or not?* He goes round the tree, sure enough, and the squirrel is on the tree; but does he go round the squirrel? In the unlimited leisure of the wilderness, discussion had been worn threadbare. Everyone had taken sides, and was obstinate; and the numbers on both sides were even. Each side, when I appeared therefore appealed to me to make it a majority.

How would you deal with this problem if you were William James? Would you come out for one side or the other or try to make peace in some way between them? Here is how James continued:

Mindful of the scholastic adage that whenever you meet a contradiction you must make a distinction, I immediately sought and found one, as follows: "Which party is right," I said, "depends on what you *practically mean* by 'going round' the squirrel. If you mean passing from the north of him to the east, then to the south, then to the west, and then to the north of him again, obviously the man does go round him, for he occupies these successive positions. But if on the contrary you mean being first in front of him, then on the right of him, then behind him, then on his left, and finally in front again, it is quite as obvious that the man fails to go round him, for by the compensating movements the squirrel makes, he keeps his belly turned towards the man all the time, and his back turned away. Make the distinction, and there is no occasion for any further dispute. You are both right and both wrong according as you conceive the verb 'to go round' in one practical fashion or the other."

Although one or two of the hotter disputants called my speech a shuffling evasion, saying they wanted no quibbling or scholastic hair-splitting, but meant just plain honest English "round," the majority seemed to think that the distinction had assuaged the dispute.[1]

Here James makes the move so useful in disputes of any kind, and especially in philosophical disputes, of asking that the meanings of key terms be clarified. The dispute in this case did not rest upon any disagreement concerning the facts,

---

[1] William James, Lecture 2, *Pragmatism* London: Longmans, Green and Co., 1907, pp. 43–45.

since both parties were in complete agreement about the actual path of the man and the behavior of the squirrel. The question was whether the expression "go round" applied to the man's path with respect to the squirrel or not. And James' answer is that the expression "go round" is open to different interpretations. Under one interpretation the man's path could be properly described as "going round," and under the other interpretation it should not be so described, and that should end the matter.

We have here an example of what has come to be known as "linguistic analysis"—a very fruitful approach to philosophical problems and, in general, to any problems involving reasoning. Our language has many features that may get us into trouble in particular cases. By understanding these features of our language we can avoid certain pitfalls. One such feature is that many words have a number of different senses or meanings. The word "premises" means the propositions in an argument on the basis of which the conclusion is drawn, and it also means a piece of land and the buildings on it. Because many words have this feature of having different meanings, puns are possible, for example: Two women arguing across the back fence may never agree because they are arguing from different premises (ouch!). Usually this feature of language does not create difficulties, because the context in which the word is used will make it clear which meaning is intended. But sometimes the context does not make it clear. Then the word or series of words may be *ambiguous;* that is, there may be two equally good ways of interpreting the word, and we may not know which way is proper. It would be James' point that "go around" is being used ambiguously, each group having in mind a different meaning of the expression.

Now, how can we use linguistic analysis in our problems concerning certainty? Some philosophers have proposed that we distinguish two senses of "certain," calling one sense "practical certainty" and the other "theoretical certainty." If we were to say of a particular belief that had a great amount of support that it was "practically certain" (the sense here of "practically" is not that of "almost" but of "for practical purposes"), we would mean that it would be foolish and irrational for a person to try to gather more evidence for the statement even if it would be most convenient to do so. By saying of that particular belief that it was "theoretically certain," we might mean that the very notion that counterevidence might come up is unintelligible and without sense. If we accept these two different senses of "certain," then we might wish to say that many of our beliefs are practically certain but that none of our beliefs are theoretically certain. For example, it would be utterly irrational for me to try to gather more evidence that I really do have a body or that $2 + 3 = 5$ or that I am not right now in severe pain. All of these beliefs are practically certain. But are they theoretically certain? Is it not at least intelligible that I might gain some information that ought to diminish my confidence in my belief that I do have a body? Suppose I knew that if someone had just now thrown a brick at me it would have gone right through what I take to be my body without meeting any resistance, or that if there were other people in this room right now they would not see my body, or that if I should try to move an object with my hands I would see what I take to be my hands pass right through it, and so on. Would not such observations as these lead me to at least the suspicion that my body was a kind of hallucination? Of course, if such things were actually to happen, I would first think I had gone insane or that something peculiar was going on around me, but from a strictly logical point of view, one possibility that would gain strength is that I did not at that moment have a body at all. Similarly, if I learn that at a meeting of great mathematicians it was concluded by all present that two plus three did not in fact equal five, should this not shake my confidence in the belief that $2 + 3 = 5$? And, to take my present belief that I am not in pain now, if I knew that I was now concentrating greatly on philosophical topics and that in the next instant my attention would weaken and I suddenly would feel the burning sensation of my cigarette getting close to my fingers, then would not my belief that I am at present not in pain be somewhat weakened by that knowledge? In all of these cases it would seem that we do not have theoretical certainty, although we might have practical certainty.

So, concerning the two-senses approach, we could conclude that there is really no dispute between the fallibilist and the antifallibilist. Each has a somewhat different conception of certainty, and according to the fallibilist concept of certainty it is quite clear that no statement is certain, whereas according to the antifallibilist conception of certainty, it is quite clear that some statements are certain. Each one is right, as he understands the concepts of certainty, and nothing more can be said on the matter. This is where many contemporary philosophers would wish to leave the matter. Even Descartes allowed that we could have "a moral assurance" where we might lack "a metaphysical certainty" (*Discourse on Method*, Part IV).

Perhaps this is where we should leave the matter, too, especially since you may by now probably be quite happy to go on to further topics. However, I think that one more comment should be made to show that the issue is not so simple as James' approach makes it seem. To return to the squirrel, I am inclined to be sympathetic to the "one or two of the hotter disputants" mentioned above by James. It is implausible to think that the verb "to go round" has the two distinct and equally important senses that James claims it does. For we do *not* mean by "going round" "being first in front of him, then on the right of him," and so forth. We would say that the earth went round the sun even if it turned out that the sun rotated on its own axis or went round in a circle so as always to present the same side to us. Furthermore, it would be easy to imagine an object rotating in such a way that I could even move in a *straight line* and yet be first in front of it, then on the right of it, then behind, and so forth, and thus never *go round* it at all. So it looks as though the proper answer should be that the man does go round the squirrel, although it is not as clear an example of going round something as the case of the man's going round the tree that the squirrel is on.

I am inclined to think that very similar remarks can be made about the analogous "solution" to the problem of certainty. I am inclined to think that the so-called sense of "certain" that we have labeled "theoretical certainty" is not a sense of "certain" at all and is not even an intelligible notion. It is, you recall, a sense in which the very notion that counterevidence might crop up is unintelligible and without sense. But for any belief one can always conceive of counterevidence cropping up. Such a supposition is never unintelligible. Therefore the notion of "theoretical certainty" suggested here does not itself make sense, nor does it therefore make sense to say of any or all statements that they can or cannot be "theoretically certain."

Well, what then is at stake in the dispute between the fallibilist and the antifallibilist? I think that two very difficult questions are still at issue here. Both of them are questions of judgment and not simply verbal. (1) No matter how much warrant a belief has, is there always further information that would increase the warrant if it were known? (2) Does the mere possibility of mistakes of various sorts, without any positive evidence that these mistakes have been committed, have the effect of decreasing the warrant for particular beliefs? I take it that the fallibilist would answer Yes to both of these questions and the antifallibilist would answer No to both of them. At present the matter is still under considerable dispute and it is not at all clear what the correct answers to these questions are. I am, myself, inclined to answer No to both. But if there is any place where fallibilism has a point, it is for philosophical conclusions like that.

7

The Problem of Perception and Our Knowledge of the External World

So far we have been discussing the question of whether anything can be known with certainty. We must now turn to the question, What are we entitled to believe at all, either with certainty or with only some degree of probability, *about the world around us?* Most people believe, at least before they have studied philosophy, that the world around them is for the most part what it seems to be—that physical objects really exist, that they can frequently be known to exist, and that they really have the properties they appear to have. Let us call this the commonsense view of the world, or as it is known in philosophy, "naïve realism."

Naïve realism immediately runs into two sorts of difficulty. Let us call the first the "argument from science." Scientific investigation of the world shows that the nature of physical objects is very different from what it appears to be. Physicists give us reason to think that the stable, enduring, solid, well-defined, colored, tangible objects around us, including our own bodies, are actually vast systems of tiny clusters of energy scattered at relatively great distances from each other, rushing about at enormous speeds, and having few, if any, of the properties that common sense tells us about. The physicists themselves say that they can hardly conceive of the kind of entities that they postulate as the fundamental basis of things. The world as it appears to common sense is a kind of illusion resulting from the peculiar facts about our own nervous systems. To take only one example, the colors that objects seem to us to have result solely from the fact that we are sensitive in a particular way to a very tiny range of electromagnetic radiation and insensitive to the rest. Were we sensitive in different ways or to different waves, as some animals are for example, the whole appearance of the world would be very different to us, and the world of common sense would be quite a different world. Science, then, indicates that the world of common sense is a set of appearances that only accidentally arise from deeper structures, which themselves never appear at all and can at best only be inferred. The real world, if it is known at all, is certainly not the world that appears to us.

We may create further difficulties for the naïve realist in a somewhat different way—a way we referred to in discussing fallibilism as the argument from illusion. Consider the dagger that Macbeth thought he saw before him. It seemed to Macbeth as if he saw a dagger there before him, but since he seemed to see it suspended in midair, he was suspicious of whether it was a real dagger he was seeing or not. Now it is clear that in this case Macbeth thought he saw a dagger, and the reason he thought he saw a dagger was that in terms of the appearances of things, he was presented with the look of a dagger, exactly that look which would have been presented to him if there really had been a dagger there suspended in midair before him. We are therefore forced to distinguish between the appearance-as-if of a dagger and the dagger itself.

From the fact that we get an appearance-as-if of a dagger, it is not guaranteed that there is a dagger there. So here again the naïve realist's identification of the appearances of things with the things themselves breaks down. Things are not always what they seem. They might never be what they seem.

Both these arguments make serious difficulties for the naïve realist. He held, you remember, that the world really is just the way it appears to be. But the argument from science and the argument from illusion both force us to admit that at least *sometimes* the appearances of things are quite different from how the things really are and, more important, that what we are aware of in the first instance are the appearances—not the objects themselves. The next natural questions are these, What are the objects themselves if not the appearances? and How are we to know them?

8

Idealism

In our search for an answer to the metaphysical question,
What is the ultimate nature of our world? and the epistemological question, How can we know our world? we will now
turn to one of the most fascinating and ingenious theories ever
devised by the mind of man—the theory of Bishop Berkeley
(born in Ireland in 1685, almost one hundred years after
Descartes' birth). It was Berkeley's thesis that only *minds*
exist and nothing else. So far as those things that are not
minds are concerned, as Berkeley put it, "their *esse* is *percipi.*"
That is to say, their being consists in being perceptions of some
mind or other. Each of us, then, is a mind, and the whole
world consists simply of a number of minds and nothing
more. Tables, chairs, the stars, in short the whole physical
world, exist only as appearances in these minds, and even our

human bodies themselves are simply appearances in our minds.

How could someone come to so astonishing a view as this? Let us return to Descartes' *Meditations*. There, Descartes began with the proof of his own existence, the *Cogito*. What was this *I?* At that point, all that Descartes could show was that it was a conscious thinking thing—in short, a mind. He could not as yet show that this mind was connected with a body, for he had to admit that the body that he seemed to have could conceivably be some sort of an hallucination or perceptual error. This much was clear to him—that it looked to him as if he did have a body and so on. That is, he had the appearances-as-if of a body. But he had to admit at that stage in his deliberations that these appearances might be deceptive. It was only after he proved the existence of a good God who would not deceive him that he had reason to think that these appearances were appearances of an actual body. Now Berkeley accepted the existence of the self as a thinking thing, the existence of God, and the existence of appearances of bodies. But he objected in a number of ways to the postulation of physical bodies, whether they be tables or chairs or living human bodies; he therefore rejected the later part of the Cartesian scheme, which involves the argument for the existence of a physical world.

Berkeley had a number of objections to Descartes' postulation of an external world of material objects. In the first place, Berkeley argued, the existence of such material objects is entirely *unverifiable*. All we are ever aware of are the appearances that come to us. We can never match these appearances against any material reality, because we cannot get to such a material reality. We can only be aware of appearances. So we can never gather evidence concerning what these appearances are supposed to be appearances of. Second, the postulation of these material objects is completely *unnecessary*. Since all we are ever aware of is appearances, all we ever have to know about is appearances. Do we want to know about the future? Yes, but not about the future behavior of material objects, since we will never observe them anyhow. What we want to know about is future *appearances*. So postulation of material objects is completely unnecessary for any of our purposes. Third, and this is Berkeley's most important point, the very notion of a material object is utterly *senseless*. What we are postulating when we postulate material objects is a something of which we could never have the slightest notion, "a something I know not what," as Locke called it. Since we could never have any experience of material objects, how could we form the slightest conception of what they are? If they have any properties, these could not be properties that enter into our experience and so could not be properties that we would have any understanding of. In short, we could not so much as form a concept of these material objects.

According to Berkeley, then, you are a disembodied mind that has from time to time not only thoughts and feelings but also perceptions of appearances of a body (which you call your own) and of many other bodies at various distances from you. When you think you are moving your finger, for example, what is happening is that in your mind there is the thought that you should move your finger, and this thought is followed more or less closely by the feelings of your finger moving and the visual appearance of it moving. Nothing is actually moving, but there are the appearances of things moving.

One question that arises at this point is the following: Why is it that the appearances I perceive tend to be *regular and lawlike* in their sequences? Why is it that when I have the thought of moving my finger, for the most part I perceive the appearance of my finger moving? Why is it that when I perceive the appearance of returning to my room, I then get for the most part the same set of appearances of the bed, desk, calendar on the wall, and so forth? What is the explanation of these recurrent regularities in the appearances I get?

If we are to explain regularities in appearance, we must postulate some underlying cause that produces them. Now, some people, at this point, might wish to appeal to the notion

of an underlying "something I know not what" that in some
way I know not how produces these appearances, and he might
wish to call such things "material objects." However, as we
have already seen, Berkeley had serious objections to such a
postulation on grounds of its unverifiability, uselessness, and
even senselessness. So if we are to postulate a cause, are there
any other alternatives to be considered? Berkeley thought
that he had an excellent alternative. Everyone knows that he
himself has a mind and that this mind can, under certain
circumstances, produce appearances. For example, I am
sure that you are capable of summoning up an image of
Raquel Welch. You can produce this image in your mind.
(You can also, I hope, put it out of your mind, and I suggest
you do so before continuing.) Here we have a familiar case
of an appearance that is produced by a mind. So, if we are
wondering how it is that appearances of material objects come
into our minds in such a regular way, if we feel that there
must be some explanation for this, if we are looking for some
cause of this regularity, then it is only reasonable to postulate
that there is some other mind at work that is producing these
appearances in our minds. What do I know about this other
mind? I know that this mind is more powerful than my mind
because when, for example, I get the appearance of falling and
the subsequent feeling of pain, I cannot by an effort of my
mind stop this appearance of falling and prevent the feeling
of pain that follows. I cannot control by acts of my own mind
most of the appearances I get. Furthermore, I know that this
mind is more intelligent and more knowing than my mind,
for appearances frequently bring me information and ideas
that my own mind could not produce. For example, I might
puzzle over a problem and be unable to solve it and then get
the solution by reading it in a book. So it becomes very likely
that there is some other mind at work in the universe that is
superior in power and knowledge to my mind and that produces the regular, coherent appearances that I get. This
superior mind I call "God." This God is, of course, only an
hypothesis. I postulate Him to give some explanation for

the regularities and coherences in the appearances that come to me. I also postulate other finite minds, like my own, to explain the appearances of other conscious beings (Berkeley never works this latter postulation out).

The full metaphysical scheme, then, is this: There are a number of finite spirits, each having thoughts, feelings, perceptions of appearances of physical objects, and so forth. Some of these occurrences are caused by the mind itself. In most cases, however, the contents of the mind are determined by a vastly more powerful and intelligent mind that is able to affect these finite minds and produce appearances in them. I am one of these finite spirits, and when I gaze at the starry heavens or at the rolling hills, I am in direct touch with the mind of God and am being directly affected by Him.

This metaphysical scheme of Berkeley's is probably not one that you yourself hold. But is it not clear that it is at least *possible* that our world might be the way Berkeley conceives it? Might not all of this be only a set of appearances in the mind, produced by some external mind? It is important to see that the world could be that way and that it could be that way without our knowing it to be that way. Once we have grasped this point, the natural question arises, How *do* we know that the world is not the way Berkeley describes it? Do we have even the *slightest* reason for thinking the world is not the way Berkeley describes it? Perhaps you know the story of Samuel Johnson, who is supposed to have said of Berkeley's theory as he kicked a large stone, "I refute him thus!" You can see how harmless a "refutation" this would be. Berkeley never denied that with the appearances of stone went the appearances of hardness and solidity, so that if you had the appearances of your foot moving toward and striking a stone, then you would get the appearances of your foot rebounding from the stone and probably the sensations of pain as well. Berkeley's theory is not to be so easily refuted. There is a similar story about Berkeley's friend Jonathan Swift, who is said to have invited Berkeley to tea one day. Berkeley found the door locked and Swift cried out from inside, "If your theory is correct, my good Bishop, you should be able to come right through that door." After pounding for a while, Berkeley was forced to go away without his tea. But of course, he never claimed that just because things like doors exist only in the mind, we have the power to banish the appearances at will. Once we fully understand his system, as Dr. Johnson and Dean Swift apparently did not, we will see that it would be very difficult to produce any reason for thinking that his theory is mistaken.

Yet there are serious difficulties in Berkeley's theory. In the first place, although there do not seem to be reasons to think it is false, there is also not the slightest reason to think it is true. On the theory's own terms, we only know appearances, and so we could never gather the slightest bit of evidence about the alleged cause—God—or about the existence of other minds. It is not really a question of accepting Berkeley's theory so much as it is a question of remaining completely agnostic about it and admitting that we just cannot know one way or the other. Second, the modern mind is most suspicious of explanations that appeal to a supernatural being, and for very good reason. It is admitted even by the devout that God's nature and His ways are unfathomable, and therefore, there is no way of using the hypothesis that God is the cause to derive any particular predictions about the future, or indeed about any events that are unknown—past, present or future. So the hypothesis that God is the cause of the observable regularities in our appearances can in no way be tested. Since it is a requirement of an acceptable explanation that it not merely explain but also be able to be independently confirmed (to distinguish it from so-called merely ad hoc hypotheses), it is reasonable to think that the postulation of a deity is not an acceptable explanatory hypothesis. Third, and connected with the last point about the comparative un-fruitfulness of the hypothesis, we may point out (just as Berkeley pointed out about the hypothesis of material things) that it is utterly unnecessary to make such a postulation. For purposes of theoretical economy and simplicity, can we not simply assume it as a fundamental fact about the nature of things that appearances simply happen to occur in fairly regular sequences? Will not this assumption suit all our human purposes? Criticisms of this sort, particularly the last, have led many philosophers to adopt the theory that is known as phenomenalism. We shall now go on to examine this theory in some detail.

9

Phenomenalism

Phenomenalism is, roughly speaking, Berkeley's idealism without God. According to phenomenalists, there are only appearances, and these appearances do not have any underlying cause, either supernatural or natural. They simply occur in regular and predictable ways.

Phenomenalism is a recent philosophy, and as such, incorporates a number of new developments. In the first place, instead of talking vaguely about appearances, theorists introduced a new concept, that of "sense-data." This term has had quite a stormy history since it was introduced early in the twentieth century; there have been many controversies about how it should be defined, whether it can be defined at all, and even whether it is a meaningful concept in any respect. There is to this very day controversy about this concept. The very existence of sense-data is still in question. It is the basic contention of the sense-datum theorist that there is something that is *common* to a case in which a man is actually seeing a dagger, a case in which a man is having an hallucination of a dagger, and Macbeth's case where he is in doubt as to whether there is a dagger that he sees or not. This common feature is alleged to be the daggerish appearance or "sense-datum." Opponents of the sense-datum view would deny that there is any relevant common element in these three cases. If there is anything common in these three cases, it is extremely difficult to say precisely what it is. However, I am inclined to think that it *is possible* to say what is common in all three cases, namely, that *to each* of the three people, *it looks as if he were seeing a dagger.* Thus, we might say that the common sense-datum in these three cases is that particular look, the look as if there were a dagger being seen. We could say of each of the people that he is having, or "sensing," a sense-datum. A "visual sense-datum" would be defined as looking to someone as if he were seeing something, a "tactual sense-datum" as feeling to someone as if he were touching something, and so forth. We may now define phenomenalism as the theory that material objects are nothing but collections of sense-data. That is to say, the real dagger is a collection of looks, feels and even sounds, smells, and tastes.

Another important innovation of phenomenalism will become relevant when we consider that many objects are only occasionally observed, and sometimes never observed. Consider your own liver, for example. It is quite likely that it will never be observed, and so there never will be any actual sense-data that will occur with respect to it. What would it mean in a phenomenalist context to say that you actually do have a liver. We have to introduce the notion of *possible* sense-data (sometimes called "sensibilia"—the looks, feels, and so forth, that people actually *would* get under certain circumstances, for example, during an autopsy. Here again, many controversies have arisen, for if the notion of a sense-datum seems difficult to grasp, the notion of a *possible* sense-datum seems even more difficult to grasp. It is like the ghost of a ghost.

But here again the notion need not be mysterious. To talk about a possible sense-datum is not to talk about an extremely abstract object; it is to talk not about an object at all but simply about what would happen under certain circumstances. For example, to return to your liver, all we mean is that if a surgeon cut an incision in the right place in the body, then it would look to him as though he were seeing a liver (let us hope, at least). We have here what is known as a "conditional assertion"—that if certain things occur, then other things will occur. There is at present in philosophy a controversy about the nature and meaning of conditional assertions, but to discuss that issue would take us too far afield. However, there is a real question here as to how these conditional statements ought to be understood.

A third innovation of modern phenomenalism involves this: that phenomenalism is taken to be a thesis not about the world or reality so much as a thesis about language, or, even more recently, a thesis about our conceptual scheme, that is, about the way in which we conceive of the world and reality. This new interpretation of phenomenalism came about in the following way: It is reasonable to think that disputes about how the world is should be decidable, to some extent at least, by going out and making observations about the world. That is to say, if someone claims that physical objects are really such and such, it ought to be possible to gather evidence about his claim by going out and examining physical objects. But it seems extremely implausible to think that Berkeley's thesis could be in any way proved by going out and observing the world. We would still be faced with the question, How are we to interpret such observations? So it looks as though something much deeper is at stake than anything that could be settled by empirical investigation. An alternative view that came to be very popular is that what is at stake is a question concerning *the very meaning* of statements about the world— particularly, in this case, statements about material objects. In other words, Berkeley's thesis can be taken as, and phenomenalism was actually put forward as, a claim about what is *meant* when we say that there is a table in the next room. It does not seem quite right to say that phenomenalism is a thesis about language, because it does not seem to be a thesis about English as opposed to some other language. It seems better to say it is a thesis about the concepts we express when we use our language, so that whether we use the English sentence or the French sentence, we will still be expressing the concept of there being a table in the next room. One final qualification is required here. It would be wildly far-fetched to interpret Berkeley's thesis as a thesis about our actual language or conceptual scheme. Almost no one takes the sentence, "There is a chair in the next room," to be a statement about God and the appearance that He is producing. So the best that can be said about Berkeley's thesis and what phenomenalists would claim for their thesis is that it is a *recommendation* as to how our language or our conceptual scheme *should* be interpreted, rather than a descriptive about the actual state of our language or conceptual scheme. The term "explication" is sometimes used here to mean a partial redefinition of a concept or set of concepts in order to introduce greater precision, efficiency, and simplicity into the language.

The thesis of phenomenalism, then, can be stated as follows: A statement about physical objects is best understood if it is understood as a set of conditional statements about sense-data.

We must now ask ourselves what can be said in favor of the recommendation of the phenomenalist. In the first place, the phenomenalist would argue that his interpretation captures much of what we do, in fact, ordinarily mean when we make statements about physical objects. When we say that there is a table in the next room, we do ordinarily mean, at least in part, that if we were to go into the next room, we would have the experiences that we would call those appropriate to seeing a table. If we talk about the nature of the far side of the moon, we are referring, at least in part, to what would be experienced by an observer if he were able to get to the far side of the moon. So it is clear that at least part of what we mean is indeed reflected in the proposal of the phenomenalist. Second, the phenomenalist recommendation captures, according to the phenomenalist, *all of what is verifiable* when we make physical-object statements. In the end, the only basis we have for making physical-object statements is the way things appear to us to be. If we wish to be cautious, if we wish not to say more than we can directly observe, then we would be wise to restrict our statements to just what can be directly observed, and nothing more. Here we can see an answer to at least one of Descartes' skeptical doubts—the doubt about the discrepancy between appearances and some underlying, unobservable reality. This doubt cannot arise if we identify reality with a consistent, coherent collection of appearances. Finally, the phenomenalist would claim that his account is perfectly clear and offers a thoroughly intelligible concept. After all, we know what appearances are, since we experience them all the time. We then simply analyze physical-object statements solely in terms of appearances. There is no mysterious component, "a something I know not what," to puzzle or baffle us. The concept of physical object has become entirely clear. If anything is missing from it, the phenomenalist would argue, it is the obscure and unintelligible elements. And nobody will miss those. In short, then, the phenomenalist claims that his recommended concept can serve all of the purposes for which the concept of physical objects is used and omit many of the obscure elements in the ordinary concept of physical objects.

Over the years many objections have been made against phenomenalism, but most of them have represented a misunderstanding of the phenomenalist's position. For example, one objection has been that according to the phenomenalist, there no longer can be any distinction between appearance and reality as this is ordinarily understood. It is claimed that according to the phenomenalist, the hallucinated dagger that Macbeth thought he saw has as much reality as an actual dagger, since in both cases it is simply a matter of appearances. The whole world then becomes nothing but a set of appearances—a kind of consistent, coherent hallucination. This objection does not carry any weight, however. The phenomenalist is quite happy to make what he claims to be a most useful distinction between appearance and reality. A real dagger, on the phenomenalist account, is a particular set of appearances that covers not only visual appearances to one person, not only the whole range of sense appearances—visual, tactual, olfactory, and so forth—to that person, but sense appearances to a large number of observers. Macbeth's "dagger" is an hallucination, on a phenomenalist's account, because it is only a small fragment of the set of appearances that would be required for a thing to be real. So the phenomenalist would call "real" exactly the same things that we would. The pink rat that the drunk seems to see would definitely only be an appearance for the phenomenalist, since there is not presented the full set of appearances that a real pink rat would present. The advantage of such a scheme, the phenomenalist would claim, is that the distinction between appearance and reality is now verifiable.

A more sophisticated version of this same criticism is that when I say there is a table in the next room, I mean that *it really exists there now,* whereas all the phenomenalist means is that there is a set of purely conditional facts, such as that if someone were there now he would have certain experiences, or, in general, if certain things happened, then other things would happen. All of these are purely hypothetical statements and, therefore, cannot have the same sense as the categorical assertion that right now there does exist in that room a particular object. The phenomenalist's reply to this objection is to raise the question, What is meant by asserting "categorically" that there is a table there now? The phenomenalist would claim that when such categorical assertions are made, they are properly interpreted in the hypothetical way he advocates. There is, of course, a *grammatical* difference between a categorical statement and a set of hypothetical statements, and the phenomenalist would admit that. But he would deny that there is anything more than this grammatical difference between them.

What is the phenomenalist to make of statements of science —for example, statements about electrons and other subatomic particles that obviously cannot be analyzed in terms of electron-appearances and the like?   Here phenomenalists tend to hold that statements about subatomic particles ought to be analyzed in terms of statements about physical objects, just as statements about physical objects ought to be analyzed in terms of statements about sense-data.   To talk about subatomic particles is to talk in a complicated way about pointer readings, certain sorts of photographic plates, cloud chambers, and the like.   We have here a pyramid in which the basic statements are sense-data statements; physical-object statements are analyzed in terms of them; and the theoretical statements of the sciences are to be analyzed in terms of physical-object statements.   How about causal assertions about physical objects?   For example we ordinarily might say that the cause of the fire was a lamp that overturned. But if the lamp is just a collection of sense-data, how could a collection of sense-data cause anything at all?   The problem here is that we must give *full* translations of physical-object statements. It is true, on the phenomenalist account, that a chair, for example, may be said to be a collection of sense-data, but this does not mean that someone could throw a collection of sense-data through a window.   The reason it would be absurd to talk about throwing a collection of sense-data through a window is that the window itself is a collection of sense-data.   So the chair's going through the window is to be analyzed in terms of the appearances of chairs, the appearances of windows, and the appearances of chairs going through windows. We cannot give a partial translation but must give a complete one.   Similarly, with causal statements, one cannot say that a collection of appearances caused a fire, but when we say that a lamp caused a fire, this is to be interpreted as a statement about the appearances of the lamp, the subsequent appearances of fire, and a law that correlates the appearances of one with the appearances of the other.   Of course, when this is all worked out in detail, it will be extremely complicated. But that is no objection against it.   Similarly, the phenomenalist does not deny that when, for example, I have a sense-datum of seeing the sun, the sun is the cause of the sense-datum.   He would simply insist that the statement must be further analyzed and then it will turn out that the sun itself is a collection of sense-data, and that under certain circumstances members of that class are correlated in a regular way with members of the class of sense-data that are my sense-data.

How about statements about the past?   Suppose I say that there was an unnoticed fire in the pantry last night.   Some critics claim that the phenomenalists must interpret this as a statement about the future—that, for example, if we go into the pantry we will find charred remains of a fire.   And this indeed would be an objection, because it would be extremely paradoxical for the phenomenalist to have to end up interpreting statements about the past as really statements about the future.   There is no need for the phenomenalist to do this.   What the phenomenalist will say here is that the conditional statements are statements about the *past*—for example, that if there *had been* an observer in the pantry, he would have seen smoke and flames. Now it is true that this does introduce the rather puzzling notion of what is called today a "contrary-to-fact conditional statement."   But many other theories involve such statements, not simply phenomenalism, so it cannot be a special objection against that theory. All of these objections, although they have been thought at one time or another to be serious objections to phenomenalism, can be met.

There is one area of objections, however, that does seem to be more threatening to the phenomenalist case.   We can get some idea of this area of difficulty if we demand of the phenomenalist that he take some physical-object statement and actually *give* us its interpretation in sense-data terms.   No phenomenalist has even been able to meet this challenge. Let us take a fairly simple statement, "I see the moon." This is a statement that all of us would understand. Now, how are we to explain the meaning of this statement in sense-data terms? Presumably, at least one thing that is entailed by this statement is that I am now getting a sense-datum of a particular sort. But what sort? A roundish, yellowish, sense-datum? Not necessarily. It may be a crescent moon or half-moon; it may be a reddish moon. It may even be a darkish moon if I am seeing it through some sort of clouds, smoke, or filter. Well, let us give the phenomenalist a break here and allow him to say that I am now having a "moonish" sense-datum. This is already a considerable concession, since it is very unlikely that there is such a thing as a moonish sense-datum. Almost anything could count as an appearance of the moon under some circumstances or other. Suppose, for example, we are all searching the skies, waiting for the moon to appear, and I see, on the horizon, just the slightest speck of light. I might say in these circumstances, "I see the moon," and be right in saying that. Yet if we are going to allow a speck of light on the horizon to count as a moonish sense-datum, then it looks as though almost any sense-datum might count under certain circumstances as a moonish sense-datum. Hence, it is unlikely that we succeed in characterizing a class of sense-data when we introduce the term, "moonish sense-data." But let us not labor this point. There are much greater difficulties for the phenomenalist.

When I say, "I see the moon," I mean a good deal more than that I am now having a moonish sense-datum. What more? Well, for one thing, I mean that if someone were here next to me he would see the moon also. But how do we specify this in sense-datum terms. Suppose, just to keep it all in the first person, we put it this way: If I were to get the sense-data as if there were a person standing next to me and the sense-data of my asking him, "Do you see the moon?" then I would get the sense-data of his nodding his head Yes, saying Yes, or the like. Perhaps we would have a whole list of conditionals of that sort involving other people, involving myself in the future, involving the past perhaps, involving views from other locations, and so forth. But one thing is now quite clear—that no finite set of such conditionals that we might write down could ever be sufficient to exhaust the meaning of "I see the moon." Any set of such conditional statements would be incomplete, and necessarily so. We can see this in the following way. No matter how many appearances-as-if of the moon we had, it would always be possible to set up a sufficiently complicated *artificial* setting in which we could get these appearances without the moon's actually being there. That is to say (remembering the argument from illusion) that illusion is always possible. The problem here is not just that the moon presents infinitely many appearances (for example, from the infinitely many points in space around it), but that these appearances are not connected in a regular way so that we could give rules for constructing the set of sense-data. The ever-present danger of illusion can never be ruled out.

But the worst is yet to come, for it is reasonable to think that we could not even write down *one* conditional. Take the conditional statement I proposed before—namely, that if I had the appearances of asking someone next to me whether he saw the moon, I would get the appearances of his saying he did. Now it is quite possible that it is true that I am now seeing the moon but that such a conditional is false. For example, suppose this person next to me is deaf. Then I might get the appearances of his being there and the appearances of asking him whether he sees the moon, but not the appearances of his agreeing with me. So I really must lengthen my conditional as follows: If I have the sense-data of asking a man next to me whether he sees the moon and if he does actually hear me, then I will get the appearances of his nodding in agreement. But now we can't just put in a phrase like "if he does actually hear me," because that is not a sense-datum phrase. What we need here is to specify his actually hearing me in sense-datum terms. Now one thing we might try is to add a little subconditional here to the effect that he has good hearing, as follows: If at this point we were to get the appearances of giving him a hearing test, we would get the appearances of his passing it. But now here again that would not show that he has good hearing (because he might cheat on the test, for example), nor would it follow from the fact that he has good hearing that this conditional would be true. For, after all, I might have misadministered the hearing test. So we would have to have another conditional in here to try to bring out the notion of my really giving him a test. And here again we would run into the same difficulty. So it seems fairly clear that we could not write down even *one* conditional sense-datum statement, since any one we started to write would become infinitely long before we could finish it. And this seems to me to be the death blow to phenomenalism—that we could not even *begin* to give the interpretation of physical-object statements that the phenomenalist thinks is the correct one.

10

Causal Theories of Perception

The last group of theories we shall consider are causal
theories. They share this in common: They postulate physical objects as *existing independently* of any observers and
having certain objective properties that characterize them.
Sense-data are the *result* of the causal interaction of these
material objects with the bodies of particular persons. The
main variations in these theories come from differing views
on the intrinsic properties of the physical objects. On some
accounts we can never have any idea what their properties
are; on other accounts they have certain unfamiliar properties (for example, charge, spin, rest-mass). On still other
accounts physical objects have some of the familiar properties
but not others; they have, for example, according to some
theories, a particular shape, size, and weight, but not any
particular color, taste, or sound. And finally, there are those

theories in which physical objects have all the familiar properties that we know of, including color, smell, and sound.
What all these theories have in common is the notion that
material things are *causes* of our experience. But these
theories must say something about the nature of the causes
if they are to be theories of *material* objects, since, as we
have seen, Berkeley also has a causal theory insofar as he
identifies God, the superior *mind,* as the cause of our experiences. We must at least say that these causes are non-
conscious and located in space. These two properties at
least are necessary in order to make these causes physical.

It is fairly clear that causal theories do better justice to the
conceptual scheme we actually have than phenomenalistic
theories or Berkeley's idealism. We certainly do ordinarily
think of material things as things that exist independently
of any observer. We believe that these things may well have
existed long before there ever were any observers and will
continue to exist even if all observers should perish. And
this does *not* mean merely that if there were observers they
would have certain experiences. This means that they would
exist quite independently of any observers at all. We believe
that a fire continues to burn in a room when we leave it, not
in the merely conditional sense that if we return we will see
a fire burning or ashes and so on, but in the sense that there
actually is a process going on during the period when no one
is there. We believe that these independent existents can
affect each other and produce changes in each other whether
they are observed or not, and that the powers to produce
these changes truly reside in them. Furthermore, it is a part
of our conceptual scheme that one and the same material
object can affect one person at different times, can affect
many different people at the same time, and can affect one
person in a number of different ways at the same time. That
is to say, it is part of our conceptual scheme that objects are
public and accessible to different people in different ways.

What is the objection, then, to the causal theory? The
major objection seems to be that there is no conceivable way

in which we could show that material objects, in the causal-theory sense, exist. Having adopted the concept of sense-data, it is plausible to think that sense-data are all we are ever aware of at first hand. If we have any information about material objects, it must be by *inference*. If our sense-datum experiences are of a certain order and regularity, we infer that there are physical objects around us of some particular sort. But the trouble with this inference is that there is no way of checking it to ensure that it is correct. We could only check that it was a correct inference if we were able to determine something about material objects independently of our sense-data. But this we can never do, since we can never get beyond the sense-data to the physical objects themselves.

As we shall see later this particular line of argument is misguided, but it is astonishing how most causal theorists have accepted it. They have conceived their task to be that of trying to *justify the inference* from sense-data to physical objects. One typical way in which this is done is to think of material objects as being like the subatomic particles of physical theory—entities that are not themselves observed but that can be to some degree verified indirectly. If we postulate the existence of certain unobservable entities having certain properties, then we can derive from these postulations certain predictions about what will be observable under certain circumstances. The theory enables us to predict things that are observable and at the same time furnishes us with an explanation of why these observable occurrences are the way they are.

Notice how far we have already moved from our commonly accepted conceptual scheme. On the causal account as here presented, we never observe the table, chairs, and other bodies around us—not even our own bodies; we simply postulate the existence of entities "out there" that somehow produce the effects that constitute our familiar world. We are indeed like the prisoners of Plato's cave—restricted solely to observing the shadows and trying desperately to infer the nature of the real objects that are casting the shadows.   This is not our ordinary conceptual scheme.

This is not to say that these departures from our ordinary conceptual scheme are necessarily deficiencies in the theory. They might well represent needed improvement.   There is no reason why we cannot take this theory to be a recommendation or "explication," just as phenomenalism can be taken. Let us see in a specific case how the causal analysis would work. Take the sentence "I see the moon." It would be recommended that this sentence be taken to be equivalent in meaning to "I am now having a visual sense-datum of a moonish sort, and this sense-datum is caused by the action of a material object called 'the moon.' "

There are some difficulties in this scheme that must be mentioned.   First there is the difficulty, noted above in connection with the phenomenalist scheme of specifying what a "moonish" sense-datum would be.   This would be no easier a problem for the causal theorist.   Furthermore, there is the problem of giving an account of the meaning of "material object" and "cause."   How are we to conceive material objects? What properties are we to give them?   Or consider the word "cause."   Hume suggested that this word should be understood to refer to an observable, constant conjunction between events, such that whenever the first is observed, the second can be observed.   It is clear that this sense of "cause" could not be applied to the relation between the purported causes, that is, the unobservable material events, and their purported effects, that is, the sense-datum events.   One could never observe their correlation.   The notion of cause will have to be a more complicated notion than that.   These latter difficulties are peculiar to *causal* accounts; questions about the conception of material objects concern the *content* of the theory postulated, and questions about the conception of causes have to do with the relationship between theoretical statements and sense-datum statements.   This raises a series of very difficult questions that are characteristically discussed in the philosophy of science. Very roughly, what we want is to be able to make inferences from a number of sense-datum statements to a number of theoretical statements; then, within the theoretical language, to infer from certain properties of theoretical objects to other properties of theoretical objects; and finally, from these new theoretical statements, to infer new sense-datum statements that will be predictions based on the theory. The test of the truth of the theory will be its usefulness in allowing us to predict and explain the occurrences of sense-data. All of this is no doubt extremely rough. It would be the obligation of the causal theorist to state all of this with much more precision. There is a real question as to whether this could be done. Certainly, no one has even begun to give a serious, detailed account.

If we cannot spell out the theory in terms of which we are to analyze material-object statements, then is not the causal theorist in the same boat the phenomenalist is in? We saw that the main objection to phenomenalism is that there is good reason to think that the meanings of material-object statements could never be in any way indicated in sense-datum terms. If it is true of causal theories that the meanings of material-object statements cannot be elucidated in theoretical terms, then causal theories also have to be rejected. However, there is the following reason to think that the causal theorist's enterprise might be able to be worked out. We already do have, in the case of, say, physics, a theory involving theoretical entities, which has shown itself to be extremely useful for prediction and explanation. We can, therefore, infer that it would be at least possible to work out a similar theory for ordinary material objects taken as theoretical entities. Certainly, this is the analogy that causal theorists have had in mind. They have argued that just as it is possible to postulate theoretical entities like electrons relative to material objects like tables and chairs, so it should be possible to think of material objects like tables and chairs as theoretical entities relative to the directly observable sense-data. We then have

some reason for thinking that the program of the causal theorist is at least a possible one.   This we did not have in the
case of phenomenalism.

We may summarize the case for the causal theory by returning to the three objections of Berkeley to the notion of a physical world.   He said that such a postulation was unverifiable,
unnecessary, and, in fact, meaningless.   The causal theorist
would claim the following: The postulation of physical objects is verifiable by virtue of the predictions it would allow us
to make concerning the future course of sense experience.
The postulation is not unnecessary, because the contents of
the theory would allow us to predict future sense-data, which
could not be predicted only on the basis of past sense-data
alone.   The key terms in the theory would gain their meaning
in part from their loose connection with sense-datum terms
and in part from their syntactical connection with other terms
in the theory.   The claim of the causal theorist is that material
objects should be considered part of a theory for explaining
sense-data just as electrons and other subatomic particles are
part of a theory for explaining material objects.

So far, we have actually said very little in favor of the causal
theory.   We have not said that it is correct or even that it is
plausible.   All we have said is that there is some reason to
think it might be possible to give a causal interpretation of
statements like "I see the moon."   But it is quite obvious that
the interpretation of this statement, if the theoretical part were
worked out fully, would be enormously complicated, and that
when we ordinarily say, "I see the moon," we do not mean anything so extraordinarily complicated.   It might be worthwhile
going back a few steps in the argument to see how the causal
account got to be so complicated.

All of this came about because the causal theorist was wor-
ried by the objection that according to the causal theory, we
would only be aware of sense-data and so could have no way of
showing that material objects exist.   His answer to this objection was that we could have some reason to think that
material objects exist if we conceived of them as theoretical

entities, since then we could be aware of them *indirectly* through inference. But this is to fall into a trap. It is to admit that all we can ever be aware of is sense-data and that we must try to show that our knowledge of material objects is somehow an inference from the sense-data we are aware of. But let us now raise the question of whether it is true that it is only sense-data that we are aware of.

How could one ever come to the conclusion that it was only sense-data we were aware of in perception? One possible route is this: First, we note that when a speaker makes a perceptual claim, for example, "I see the moon," he implies that it looks to him as if he were seeing the moon. This implication may be stated as "I am having a moonish sense-datum." Now, suppose I am having a hallucination, and there is no moon there at all; that is, suppose I just look up into an empty sky and seem to see the moon. What am I then seeing? At this point it becomes very tempting to say that since I am not seeing an object there, the only thing left for me to be seeing is the moonish sense-datum. And now the sense-datum has become a kind of object—a something that can be seen. Then, noticing that even when the moon is really there I still have a moonish sense-datum, it becomes tempting to think that even when the moon is there, what I am actually seeing is the moonish sense-datum and not the moon at all. So when I say, "I see the moon," I am, strictly speaking, simply seeing the moonish sense-data and inferring that there is a moon there. Hence, the conclusion that we never see material objects, only sense-data. Put a little less objectionably, we might say that we are only aware of physical objects by virtue of inferring them from sense-data. We are now in the trap, and we must thrash around frantically to find some way of explaining our knowledge about material objects. On the causal account, they are theoretical inferences.

But this is all a tissue of absurdities. In the first place, it is a mistake to think that we *see* sense-data. At best we must say that we *have* sense-data. But even this is a misleading way of saying that it sometimes seems to us as though we were seeing an object. To slide from "I seem to see the moon" to "I am seeing a seeming moon" would be like going from "I seem to be walking down the stairs" to "I am walking down the seeming stairs." Furthermore, even if we understand the sense in which when it looks to us as though we were seeing the moon, we may say, "I am seeing a moonish sense-datum," it still hardly follows that when we actually see the moon, all we are really seeing is the moonish sense-datum. The reason for making this move, you remember, was that when there was no moon there, it seemed plausible to say, "I am seeing *something*," so we said, "I am seeing a moonish sense-datum." But why should we think that even when the moon is there, all we are seeing is a moonish sense-datum? We were lead to say that we were seeing a moonish sense-datum precisely because there was no *moon* there to be seen. So when there is a moon there to be seen, it is absurd to say that we are seeing only a moonish sense-datum and inferring the existence of the moon. If it is a cloudy night and I catch glimpses of bits of light occasionally in the sky, I might then *infer* that the moon is there; but if it is a clear night and the moon is shining brightly in the sky, it would be absurd to say that I infer the moon. I see it plainly. Of course, I might be wrong. I might be drunk, hallucinating, or otherwise deluded. If so, I would think I saw the moon, but I would not have seen it. But it does not follow from the possibility of delusion that I never see the moon. Sometimes, when I am sober and undeluded, I see it quite plainly, and I am quite sure that all of you have also seen the moon from time to time.

Once we are tricked into thinking that the moon is an inference, then the problem is to justify the inference, and we may find ourselves driven to accept the causal account. Notice that the phenomenalist also may be tempted to hold this theory because he, too, has fallen into the same trap and believes that all we are ever aware of is sense-data. The phenomenalist does not wish to allow inferences to entities that are radically different from sense-data, so he construes material objects simply as a class of sense-data and construes the inference not as an inference to some theoretical entity, but as an inference to further sense-data of a particular sort.

This is not to say that phenomenalism and causal theories are utterly misguided. For there still remain the following problems: First, what is the proper analysis, if any, of perceptual statements like "I see the moon"? Or, put more generally, what are material objects, and what is it to perceive them? This is a metaphysical question. Second, how are perceptual statements and material-object statements to be justified? This is the epistemological question. And in both cases, how do sense-data come in? It is possible that phenomenalism, or some variant of the causal theory, might be helpful to us in answering such questions, but they no longer seem to be inevitable, although rather desperate, alternatives. In fact, once we have gotten away from the notion that we must start with sense-data for our analysis, then it might even become plausible to analyze sense-datum statements in terms of material-object statements. That is to say, we might start with the notion of "I see the moon" as the basic notion, and explain "moonish sense-data" as the cases in which it merely seems to us that we are seeing the moon. This seems to be the way we actually learn our language, and it might be a clue to the proper analysis of these terms.

To conclude this discussion of the problem of perception, let me offer some suggestions as to how perceptual terms might be analyzed. When I say, "I see the moon," some of the things I mean to assert are these: (1) I believe that the moon exists out there. (2) It now looks to me as if I were seeing the moon. (3) I believe that at least part of the cause of its looking to me as if I were seeing the moon is that the moon is out there. That is to say, if I thought that the cause of its looking to me as if I were seeing the moon were some kind of post hypnotic suggestion, some direct stimulation of my brain, or the effect of some drug, then I would not believe I was really seeing the *moon*. This would be so even if I happened to believe the moon was out there before me. So it looks as though there is some causal element involved in our understanding of the expression "I see the moon." Of course, none of this is decisive against phenomenalism, since the phenomenalist could accept (1), (2), and (3), but he would simply give each one of them a phenomenalistic interpretation. Nevertheless, this is some reason for preferring the causal account, since we seem to be forced to include some causal elements in our analysis, whereas the further phenomenalistic analysis seems quite gratuitous, in addition to the other difficulties we have seen in connection with it. This is not to say that we must accept that part of the causal theory which treats material objects as *theoretical* entities. We would only be forced to do that if we took material objects to be unobserved. But I have argued that there is no reason to think that physical objects are unobserved; we observe them frequently. So that feature of causal theories does not seem very plausible.

How is the topic of perception, which we have just concluded, related to our earlier topics—the problem of certainty in particular? One relationship is this. We saw that sense-datum statements, which are special cases of what was earlier called "introspective reports," have a special superiority over material-object statements as far as certainty is concerned. It is not that sense-datum statements are *more* certain than material-object statements. After all, the statement "It looks as if I were seeing an eleven-pointed mauve star" is not always more certain than the statement "I have a body." But sense-datum statements *are* superior to material-object statements in that there is one way in which the latter can go wrong, but the former cannot—namely, in the occurrence of a discrepancy between how things appear and how things are. Since sense-data are, in effect, the appearances themselves, there is no distinction to be made between the appearances and how the appearances appear. But in the case of material objects, there is a distinction to be made between the objects and how they appear, and therefore, discrepancies can arise. So the Cartesian doubt that I may be deceived because of dreaming, hallucinations, and so forth, can arise in the case of material objects but cannot arise in the case of sense-datum statements. Therefore, if we wish to start our knowledge of the external world with a more bedrock or basic sort of statement, we should start it with sense-datum statements. We then might wish to reconstruct the rest of our knowledge as inferences from sense-data. How this is to be done, or whether it can be done at all, is not clear, but both phenomenalism and causal theories present at least schematic outlines of how such analyses should proceed. Whether they are at all necessary is still another question, and if we allow that we frequently do observe material objects, it is not clear what the point of such analyses might be, as we have seen. But now we must try to see a little more clearly what the nature of these "introspective reports" is, how they are related to the self, and how the self might be related to the body.

11

The Self

We have been considering at length the question whether there is a material world and how it might be constituted. There is a celebrated passage in Descartes' second *Meditation* where he considers a piece of wax. (In those days every well-equipped desk had a piece of wax on it for hard-working thinkers to play with—and seal letters too.) Descartes notices that as he moves the wax near the fire, it begins to change its qualities; it melts, changes its shape, loses its hardness, and so forth. He finds he hardly knows what this changing object is, or whether it exists at all. But he says that whether it exists or not, he certainly *thinks* that it exists and therefore, it is at least certain that *he* exists. Here we have another application of his *Cogito*. The material world may not exist; it may all be an illusion. But he at least is quite certain that he exists. We must now turn to this "he," to this self, that does certainly exist. How should we define it?

One way to go about it is to ask which characteristics, when ascribed to the self, will allow the *Cogito* to work as a proof of its existence. For example, it might do to define the self as a thing that has sense-data, for I can be certain that it seems to me that I see something, or feel something, or taste something, and therefore I can be certain that I exist. The self can be defined as a thing that doubts, for if I doubt something, I can be certain that I doubt, and therefore, that I exist. It can be defined as a thing that believes; feels pain and other sensations; has thoughts, hopes, and fears; and so on. Descartes summed all of this by saying that the self is, in its essence and at the very minimum, a thing that thinks, or a thinking thing, by which he meant a thing capable of sensations, thoughts, sense-data, and so forth. Sometimes Descartes called it a "soul"; sometimes he called it a "mind." He intended these terms to have the same meaning, and we will treat them as the same meaning also. We shall call the changes that occur in this thinking thing (that is, its having a thought, sensation, or sense-datum) "mental events."

What is the basic characteristic of a mental event—that feature that makes it a mental event? Consider the statement "I am now in pain." This is the report of what we here call a mental event. We have already considered whether such reports, referred to in section 4 as "introspective reports," can be certain. To bring out its special feature, let us compare my saying of myself, "I am in pain" with someone else's saying of me, "He is in pain." Now, when another person says it of me, he says it on the basis of certain observations he makes. Perhaps he has seen the trunk fall on my foot, has noticed me turn white, has heard me cry out, and has seen me hopping around on one foot and clutching the other foot. In such a case it would be reasonable for him to say of me, "He is in pain." He could be quite confident of this judgment, and perhaps he might even be said to know it for certain in some circumstances. But it is clear that he knows it on the basis of observations he has made. Now, just as he has good reason to believe that I am in pain, so also do I have good reason to believe that I am in pain. But I do not believe that I am in pain by virtue of any observation I make of the trunk falling on my toe, of my jumping around, or of my nursing my foot. I know I am in pain, and my belief that I am in pain is justified on a quite different basis. This basis is *not* anything I see or hear or otherwise perceive through my senses, nor is it any inference I made. I am justified in believing it simply on the basis of being the person to whom the pain has occurred. To have the pain is itself sufficient justification for my believing I have it. And this is true for all mental events. Simply to have a particular thought puts me in the position of being justified in believing that I do have that thought. And the same goes for the having of sense-data, feelings of fear, and so forth. Not that I can't be wrong in describing them; I can. As noted in the discussion of certainty, introspective reports might be erroneous, for example, in cases of inattentiveness or lack of practice in making certain discriminations. But when they go wrong it is not because the appearances mislead us as to the reality, as might be the case if some other person were *pretending* to be in pain and on the basis of our observations we said, mistakenly, that he was in pain. Observations can always go wrong in that way. But I do not know that I am in pain on the basis of such observation, and so that way of going wrong is not present here. I may be wrong about my present experience, but I cannot be *deceived* about it. And I cannot be deceived because deception can only arise in the case of observation (where the observation may be deceptive as to the real nature of the thing observed), whereas I know of my own present experiences without having to make such observations.

But what is the "I" which has these mental events. Here we come to one of the deepest and most baffling problems in philosophy. Is that "I" merely a body, as the materialist wishes to say? Or is my body simply one aspect of my self? Or am I separate and distinct from my body, as Descartes wished to say? We must now go into these theories in some detail. They are not the only theories, but they are the most seriously considered today.

12

Materialism

Materialism, a theory that was even popular in ancient Greece, is the view that the only things in existence are material—nothing exists but "atoms and the void." Thus, the "I," or self, must be purely material.

But what are we to make of what we have called here "mental events," for example, having thoughts, feelings, sense-data? Surely some account has to be taken of them. One materialistic solution to this problem is known as behaviorism—the analysis of mental events as particular sorts of *behavior* of particular sorts of bodies. Take pain, for example. The behaviorist would claim that to be in pain is simply to behave under certain circumstances in certain sorts of ways, or at least to be disposed to act in those ways. To say a person is in pain is to say he has a tendency to turn pale, writhe, cry out, and so forth. Part of this behavior is natural. Part of it is learned, as is indicated by the familiar fact that cries of pain differ from one society to another. What of the report, "I am in pain"? Is this not a *report* of some inner mental event? No, says the behaviorist. This is just another kind of behavior—in this case, learned behavior.

Behaviorism has a certain plausibility when we consider it as a theory about *other* people. For when we say of someone else that he is in pain, the images that come to our mind and the observations we expect to make are those of a person crying out, writhing, and so forth. But it has seemed to most reflective people that behaviorism can hardly be applied to *oneself*. When I am in pain, I may very well behave or be disposed to behave in certain ways. But I know in my own case that something much more is involved, namely, some sort of internal, nonbehavioral event that we call the having of pain. It is for this reason that behaviorism has been abandoned. The only place where it can be found at all is in certain areas of experimental psychology. Even there, behaviorism exists in a very watered-down condition. As a rule, its function is limited to guiding research that says that only what can be manifested in behavior should be studied by psychologists. Since this is a rule for doing psychology, it is often known as methodological behaviorism to distinguish it from the behaviorism we have been discussing. The latter is sometimes called logical behaviorism. It is not a proposal about what should be investigated in psychology, but a metaphysical claim about the ultimate nature of mental events themselves— namely, the claim that mental events are nothing but dispositions to behave in certain ways.

A more plausible version of materialism is the theory that is known today as the identity theory. According to this theory, mental events are identical with bodily events—as it turns out, brain events. The essential feature of this theory concerns the question of what is meant here by "identical." Other examples of the sort of "identity" here intended are the discovery that the Morning Star is *identical* with the Evening Star, that water is *identical* with H_2O, and that lightning is *identical* with a particular sort of electrical discharge. Such discoveries are empirical discoveries that for a long time remained unknown. Similarly, for mental events it is held that although the identity of mental events with brain events was for a long time unknown and still is not certain, it is at least fairly probable that they are identical. In this sense the identity tñeory rests upon certain empirical results and could be overthrown by new empirical results. The actual empirical results that this theory depends upon are certain very close correlations between mental events and brain events. The philosophical aspect of the theory is that it proposes that these correlations be taken in the same way as the correlations of Morning Star with Evening Star, water with H_2O, and lightning with electrical discharges—that is to say, as the discovery of identity.

There are two objections that are currently being made to the identity theory: (1) Brain events occur in a particular spatial location, whereas it is nonsensical to say that mental events occur in any particular spatial location. What would it mean to say that I just had a thought that occurred two inches behind the bridge of my nose, or that I just had a sensation of fear midpoint between my ears, or that I just had a sense-datum of a red patch two inches behind my eyeballs? Since it makes no sense to give mental events this sort of spatial location, they cannot be identical with events that do have that sort of spatial location—namely, brain events. So, the identity cannot hold. (2) Brain events are public events, in principle observable by anyone whatsoever, whereas mental events are private events, in the sense that the person to whom a mental event occurs stands in a very special and privileged position with respect to that event. The special position is this, that if he firmly believes he has that mental event, then he cannot be mistaken in that belief, the belief must be correct. Necessarily, if a person firmly believes that he is feeling pain, then he is feeling pain. Here mental events differ from brain events. If a person firmly believes that he is undergoing some brain event, he may still be mistaken about it. Since mental events have this element of what is currently called "privileged access" and brain events lack this element, they cannot be identical.

How are we to account for these two differences between mental and physical events?   We postulate that they are separate and distinct events, both occurring in the same time series, perhaps, but the latter occurring in the spatio-temporal world while the former do not.   This view seems quite plausible once the differences between the mental and the physical have been called to our attention.   Imagine your being hit on the head in such a way that you have the visual experience we call "seeing stars."   Now we would all agree that the blow to your skull is a purely physical event.   It is clear that this has an effect on your brain that involves various sorts of shakings and jarrings of various parts.   This may lead to certain electrochemical changes in the part of your brain that is known as the visual cortex.   All of this is physical in a perfectly straightforward way, and a physiologist might be familiar with the sorts of changes that might be going on.   If your brain were magnified a thousand times, or if we had special high-powered microscopes, we might be able to observe all of these changes in great detail.   But one thing *we* could not observe, and one thing that *you* are directly aware of without having to make any observations through microscopes, is the flash of color and light that we call "seeing stars."   *We* may *infer* that that event took place, and *you* may, by your later behavior, indicate that it took place, but that particular event is a mental event and utterly different from any physical event we might observe.   And no materialistic theory, however ingeniously defended, will convince us otherwise.   It looks as though we must admit the existence of mental events as something different from physical events.   To admit this is to admit the need for some sort of dualistic theory—that is, a theory that allows both mental events and physical events.   We might note that Berkeley's idealism, in allowing the mental but not the physical, is not dualistic.   However, as we have seen, ideal-

ism is in its own monistic way as implausible as the extreme
materialism is in its monistic way.

Some philosophers have admitted the distinction between
the mental and the physical but have held that each is simply
a different aspect of some *one underlying thing.* Hence such
theories are sometimes called double aspect theories. The
most famous double aspect theorist was Spinoza, who held that
a man has two quite different aspects to him—his physical and
his mental aspects. The analogy is sometimes used of an un-
dulating line that at any particular time might be concave
from one point of view and convex from the other point of
view; each of these would be a different aspect of one and the
same thing—the line. Double aspect theories have some serious
difficulties. For one thing, there is the question of the nature
of this underlying thing that has the two aspects. In Spinoza's
case, it was extremely obscure. He called it "substance," and
he held that substance has infinitely many aspects, although
the mental and the physical are the only ones we know. He
also called it "God or nature." How obscure this notion of
substance is can be brought out by the fact that to this very
day there is great controversy as to whether Spinoza was an
atheist or, as a later commentator called him, "a God-
intoxicated man." Another double aspect theorist, Herbert
Spencer, put his cards on the table in referring to this underlying reality simply as "the unknowable." In recent times,
some philosophers have suggested that the underlying unity
might be taken to be "the person." But when one inquires
what a "person" is, it looks as though the most that can be
said is that it is the sort of thing that has both a physical and
a mental aspect. And this puts us back at the beginning, so
far as trying to find out what the underlying reality is.

A second difficulty for a double aspect theorist is trying to
clarify the meaning of "aspect." In the case of the moving
line that is convex and concave, it is quite clear what "aspect"
means; it means spatial viewpoint or place from which the
line is observed. But this simple sense, spatial viewpoint, is

not applicable to the underlying reality of which the mental and the physical are supposed to be aspects, so it is not clear what "aspect" means in that case. Some contemporary philosophers suggest that we talk of the physical as the thing as seen "from the outside," and the mental as the thing as seen "from the inside." But presumably this is not meant to be taken literally. I am not sure how things would look from inside my brain, but presumably, things would be pretty dark, to say the least. If we are not to take "from the inside" and "from the outside" literally, if we are to take these expressions in some metaphorical way, then this still remains to be clarified.

A third difficulty emerges if we turn on consideration to physical objects, such as rocks. Now Spinoza held that rocks also have two aspects—a physical and a mental—as do all things in the universe. Spinoza thought that *every* physical entity has a corresponding mental aspect; this view is called "panpsychism." It has never struck very many philosophers as a plausible position. But what is the alternative? If we say that a rock is merely physical, then we will be committed to a basic difference between the bodies of things that also are thinking things and all other bodies. So far as conscious things are concerned, their being physical will only be an aspect of something else, let us call it a "person." But in the case of a rock, its being physical will be the basic characteristic of it. So rocks and persons are in principle quite different sorts of things. Thus we are forced back into dualism of two basically different kinds of stuff or things, a dualism that the double aspect theory was originally designed to eliminate but fails to do.

13

Mind and Body

We have considered various materialistic attempts to identify mental events with material events—with either certain sorts of behavior of material objects or with particular sorts of events in those material objects. These theories have all had serious defects. It seems reasonable to think that mental events cannot be construed as material. We must think of them as something separate and distinct from, something over and above, the body. If so, two questions must be raised here: How are these events related to the body? and How are they related to each other? In this section the first of these two questions will be discussed, and in the following section the second will be discussed.

Three theories have gained prominence as accounts of how mental events are related to the body. The first of these, epiphenomenalism, takes mental events to be mere *by-*

products of bodily activity, particularly brain activity. This can be taken to be a materialist theory in a somewhat extended sense of that term, since the claim is that the material world is the basic world, and mental events are mere causal results of material changes. The French physician Cabanis gave expression to this view when he said that the brain secretes thought just as the liver secretes bile. Less pungent analogies that have been used by epiphenomenalists are the relationship between a body and its shadow and between a steam locomotive and the steam that issues from its funnel. According to this view, thoughts, sensations, sense-data, and the like have no effects on anything; they are mere consequences of what happens in the brain.

A somewhat different theory is known as interactionism. The interactionist admits that in many cases mental events are mere consequences of things that happen in the body. For example, when a trunk falls on my toe, the various changes that go into my body result in the mental event that we call pain. Again, when light reflected from the moon affects my visual system, there results the mental event we have called the having of a moonish sense-datum (see the causal theory, discussed in section 10). To this extent, the interactionist agrees with the epiphenomenalist. But the interactionist holds that in some cases, at least, mental events are able to produce effects on the body. Thus he would hold that when a man winces from pain, the occurrence of the mental event that is the having of the pain affects the body in such a way as to produce the wince. Again, if I have a thought of which I am ashamed, this may cause my cheeks to turn the characteristic reddishness that we call blushing. Again, excessive worry may produce changes in the body that result in the pathological condition we refer to as ulcers. Descartes was an interactionist and he even had a theory of what part of the brain was the crucial point at which mental events and the brain interact. Because it was at the center of the brain, the pineal gland was chosen as the point of interaction; although there is no evidence that Descartes was right about this, to this very day the function of that particular part of the brain is still a mystery.

One important way in which mental events are supposed to affect the body, according to the interactionist theory, is found in the case of volitions, or acts of will. It is held that when I make up my mind to do something, for example, wink at the girl across the table from me, the mental event of deciding to wink has the effect of producing the particular facial change we call a wink. It is here that room is left for "free will," since no information about the body is sufficient for us to be able to predict that the wink will occur. The cause of the wink is not some prior bodily state, but a mental event. So the wink would be considered, from the point of view of the physical world alone, a random, that is, uncaused, change. But, of course, it would have a cause, namely, a mental cause. Someone who believed in "free will" might find this a reason for preferring the interactionist theory.

A third important theory of accounting for the relation between mental events in the body is parallelism. The parallelist repudiates the notion that there can be a *causal* connection between mental events and the brain either going only from brain to mental events or going both ways. How can events so utterly dissimilar, he asks, possibly affect each other? Deciding that causal connection is impossible, the parallelist holds that every mental event is merely *correlated* with some physical event in such a way that whenever the one occurs then the other occurs also. Leibnitz offered the analogy of two perfect clocks that are so synchronized when they are constructed that they remain forever in phase without any further adjustments. Thus, whenever one strikes midnight, the other strikes midnight. There is no causal connection, because each has its own inner works, but the states of each mechanism are always correlated with particular states of the other mechanism. Thus, to take some of our earlier examples, whenever my brain is in that state produced by a trunk falling on my toe, then my mind is in the parallel state of feeling pain; similarly, when my mind is in the state of having decided to wink at the girl across the table, my brain is always in the parallel state of starting the chain of events that will eventuate in my winking.

So far as deciding between these three theories is concerned, I believe we can pretty easily eliminate the last of them, parallelism. There does not seem to be any explanation to account for the constant conjunction of the mental and the physical, and to take it as a mere accident seems too farfetched to take seriously. But whether we incline towards epiphenomenalism or interactionism depends upon whether or not we take the brain to be a relatively closed system whose changes can be fully explained in terms of prior physical events. If we were to extrapolate from the recent history of physics, with its trend toward encompassing wider and wider ranges of phenomena, we might give the edge to epiphenomenalism. But if we hold that changes occur in the brain that cannot be explained in terms of prior physical events but that require the postulated intervention of mental events, then we are opting for interactionism. The sad fact is that it is still too early to tell. We may just have to wait about a hundred years before the outcome is more decidable. And if, at the end of that time, we still do not have a general theory of the brain that will, in principle, explain all, we still will not have settled the matter, for the epiphenomenalist can still say we must continue to search for such a theory. Or he can say that some brain events just occur at random. So we cannot expect much in the way of decisiveness here, unless we do come upon a general theory of the brain that will explain all, in which case then epiphenomenalism will have triumphed.

14

The Mind

So far, we have seen that there exists a series of mental events, thoughts, sensations, sense-data, and so forth, that are connected with the body either causally or by regular correlations. These mental events are not only related to the body, however; they are also related to each other. For it is correct to describe these mental events as all *of the same mind*. It still remains for us to discuss the question of what the nature of the mind is, the "I" that is the subject of Descartes' "I think therefore I am." What is this "mind" that all these mental events belong to? One theory, going back to Plato, is that these mental events are events that happen to one and the same underlying, enduring, nonphysical thing. The view is often called the mental substance theory. It is the mental substance that allegedly undergoes the mental events and is related in some manner to the body.

It is very hard to give any sense to this notion of a mental substance. If I look inward and search the contents of my mind, I don't seem to find any such thing there. Nor *could* I find such a thing there, since all I can find are mental events, and this thing is presumably the thing that is *having* the mental events. So it cannot itself be observed. It is the thing that thinks. And it seems that nothing more than that can be said. It seems doomed to lie in permanent obscurity, lurking in the background, never appearing.

Because of the obscurities in the notion of a mental substance, some philosophers have been attracted to a view first put in its modern form by Hume—that the mind is not some *underlying thing* that produces thoughts, but rather, simply, the bundle or collection of thoughts themselves. This theory is therefore sometimes called the bundle theory of the mind. Your "mind" is simply the collection of mental events you have had in your lifetime, not some mysterious, underlying, unobservable thing. You are not, of course, any particular mental event, but the whole collection of them. Since the collection extends over time, so you extend over time. When the collection ceases to have new members added to it—that is to say, when you cease having mental events—that will be the end of that collection, and so the end of you.

This is a very attractive view, since it avoids the metaphysical obscurities of the mental substance theory. But there are some problems still to be worked out here. The main question is, How are we to describe the relations between these events that make them all members of *one and the same* collection? After all, there are many more mental events occurring in the world than those that go to make up *your* mind. By what right do we rule these others out as not being proper members of the collection that go to make up your mind? One suggestion is that the contents of each individual mind are related by *memory,* in the sense that if any particular mental event is a member of the collection, then the collection will also contain subsequent memories of the earlier mental events. This as it stands is inadequate, since there are many mental events that I have that are never remembered later on. So we must say something like this. An event would be a member of a collection if it *could* be remembered later on. But one problem here is the sense of the word "could." For example, suppose that I had some unpleasant experience in my childhood that I have repressed, so that in some sense or other I "cannot" remember it. Surely this is not the relevant sense of "could." How about some of the early experiences of my childhood that occurred when I was so young that no matter how hard I tried, no matter how much psychoanalysis I had, and even, perhaps, no matter how much hypnosis or drugs I had, I still could not remember them? Would they still count as mental events in *my* mental life? And what is a memory, anyhow? Suppose it is simply a later mental state that resembles some earlier mental state and, perhaps, has the added feature of "this is familiar," or something like that (as Hume held). Then we run into the following difficulty. Take the familiar experience of *déja vu*—the experience in which it seems quite certain that we have been through something before, although it is unlikely we have. Now suppose *someone else* had had that experience before—presumably, someone else has been in that room before. Then are we remembering *his* past experience? In this case his experience is a part of our mind. But that is absurd. So there are difficulties in the notion of memory here. At any rate this is a matter with which the most recent philosophical work has concerned itself, and still nothing very clear has been forthcoming.

Finally, one last account may be suggested. Some philosophers hold that the unity of the mind consists neither in any relations among the mental events themselves nor in their relations to some mental substance, but simply in their relationship to the body. Now we do have a fairly clear idea of what it is for a body to be one and the same body for a period of time. Of course it is not exactly the same; I don't have exactly the same body I had ten years ago or even ten minutes ago. But we have some idea of what we mean when we say it is the same body—namely, that there is a certain continuity of change, and there are some relatively unchanging parts. So why not say that a series of events belong to the same mind, if all of these events are connected with the same body? The exact form of the connection would depend upon which theory of the relationship between mind and body we accept. That is, we might say of certain mental events that they were the mental events of the same mind if they were the effects of or correlated with one and the same particular brain. Thus, we would be able to find the unity of these mental events in their being related to a single enduring physical body. Such an account has seemed very attractive to philosophers, because we then do not have to seek the unity of the mind in some mysterious mental substance, nor do we have to face the baffling problem of specifying the relations between mental events that make them events of the same mind. We already know about the body and its relative unity, so that it becomes convenient to use the body as our peg on which to tie the bundle of mental events.

This attractive theory has the following consequence, however, which we must go on to discuss. It has the consequence that it rules out and renders utterly meaningless the possibility that the mind might continue to exist after the death of the body and the possibility that the mind might move from one body to another. Since each mind gains its existence as a unity from its connection with some particular body, it no longer can exist as a unity when that connection is severed. So the very notion of a mind existing without a connection to a body is unintelligible. To say that Jones' body was destroyed but his mind continued to exist would be to contradict onself, since Jones' mind is *defined* as those mental events connected with particular events in his body.

But the notion of survival of the self after the death of the body is *not* unintelligible or self-contradictory. You can imagine the situation of witnessing your own funeral. Imagine that you suddenly have a terrible pain in your chest; everything grows dim, and then there is blackness. The next thing you know you seem to be observing a scene in which a body that looks just like yours is sprawled on the floor. People are rushing around, calling for doctors, wringing their hands, and shouting your name. Finally, after a lot of confusion, the doctor stands over the body, shakes his head, and says, "I have done my best but he is gone now." You seem to see and hear all of this from a point near the ceiling, but you get no visual appearances of your own body directly beneath that point, nor do you have any of the bodily sensations you usually have. You find yourself having all sorts of thoughts and emotions, and finally the thought flashes through your mind that you are dead. But, remembering Descartes, you quickly utter a few *Cogitos* and prove that although your *body* is dead and you no longer are connected with it, nevertheless *you still exist*.

Do such things happen? Well it must be admitted that we do not really know whether they happen or not. We have shown that it is not self-contradictory to assert that they happen, but whether they do or not is an empirical question. My own view is that they most probably do not occur. The evidence I would cite is the already known intimacy of connection between mental events and brain events. We know that when certain parts of the brain are damaged, a pathological mental condition is produced, and if particular parts of the brain are totally destroyed, there may well be a total loss of mental function of a particular sort. All of this makes it likely, by inductive extrapolation, that when the brain is totally destroyed, the mind is destroyed with it. However, this sort of empirical argument is not as yet very strong. There are enormous numbers of things we are in ignorance about concerning the brain and its correlated mental functions. We know that large portions of the brain can be affected (and even removed) with hardly any noticeable difference in mental functioning. We know that in some cases of brain damage there is temporary loss of mental functioning that then, astonishingly enough, is regained. Even memories lost on removal of a part of the brain may come back again in time. So any arguments about the degree of correlation of mind and brain based upon present knowledge are not going to be very strong. It is entirely conceivable that when the brain is destroyed in death, there is a temporary loss of mental functioning, but not a permanent one. So survival of the mind after the death of the body still remains to some degree an open question.

Let us briefly consider the possibility of transmigration— the movement of the mind, or self, from one body to another. Let us see if we can imagine a case. Suppose two men are pruning a tree, and the tree is suddenly hit by lightning. Both men are knocked unconscious, and when they come to, each, with great astonishment, cries out that his body is a completely different one from the one he used to have. From each body issue forth claims about the past of the other and knowledge of facts that only the other person could have had. We also find a complete exchange of personality traits. If this exchange were carried out in complete detail, would we not be inclined to say, despite the irregularity of it all, that the two persons had somehow exchanged bodies? I think we would. So transmigration also is not self-contradictory. So far as the question of whether it ever occurs is concerned, here I should think it is almost certain that it never has occurred. In the few cases where it was claimed to have happened (for example, the "Bridey Murphy" case), more plausible explanations have always been found, such as repressed memories, hysterical changes of personality, and even fraud. So although transmigration of this sort remains a possibility, it almost certainly never happens. Still it is not self-contradictory or unintelligible to say that it has happened, and that shows that if someone presents a good deal of evidence that it has happened, we are obliged to consider the matter with care.

The possibility of such cases shows that the unity of the mind cannot be located in the unity of the body. They show that, in Descartes' words, "it is certain that this I is entirely and absolutely distinct from my body, and can exist without it" (sixth *Meditation*). This forces us back to the earlier question, What is this "I" or self, that can exist separately from the body? It reminds us of the deeper mysteries that lie behind the argument of Descartes that we mentioned at the very beginning of our investigations into metaphysics and epistemology. It seems so simple, transparent, and unquestionable to be able to say, "I think therefore I am." Such a statement may well be true, perhaps even certain, but its sense may well be extraordinarily difficult to grasp.

15

Values and Choice

So far, we have been considering a number of questions concerning the nature of reality and our knowledge of it. We examined whether, in general, anything can be known for certain, and if so, what. We then turned to an examination of the nature of the physical world and the place of the conscious self in that world. In approaching our next topic, we can appeal to a distinction expressed by Hume—the distinction between *is* and *ought*. We can say that we have been considering some questions concerning *how things are,* whereas now we will consider some questions concerning *how things ought to be*—questions in the sphere of ethics, or moral philosophy.

The field of ethics is concerned with the study of the right and the good; it seeks to determine such things as the kinds of life that are good, the kinds of people who are good, the goals and actions that have value, what the right things for people to do are, and the meaning and value of life. These questions are the most important questions we face in our lives, although very few people ever give them the systematic thought they deserve. In this brief introduction, we cannot expect to make very much progress in deciding upon the best responses to such questions. But we can *begin* the task. I shall note a few important distinctions that I believe to be important in carrying your thinking on in fruitful directions. The rest will be up to you.

A great deal of what falls into the category of *how things are* comes to pass whether we like it or not. But some of what is in that category is under our control. By our decisions and acts of will, we sometimes can affect how things are and can change them to conform more closely to our own desires and ideals. To some extent our decisions do make a difference not only to our own actions, but, like a stone dropping into a pond, to a constantly expanding chain of surrounding events. We have already mentioned the phenomenon of acts of will (volitions) causing bodily changes as an alleged example of mind-body interaction (see page 83). But *any* mind-body theory must allow that decisions can affect the way things are. We might just mention here the problem of freedom of the will: Do our acts of will themselves result from events that, in the end, lie outside our control? If so, then we ourselves, although indeed affecting things, are merely pawns through which the more basic forces of history work—we are not originators of change, but merely intervening media transmitting changes. To one who knew the forces acting upon us, we would be as predictable as dominoes in a row; each domino does have an effect, to be sure—making the next one fall, but each is completely determined to produce that result by the forces acting on it. Or, on the other hand, do our acts of will originate within ourselves? Are they spontaneous creations of the self, or perhaps even totally unpredictable, utterly uncaused, random happenings? Although this is a very difficult and important philosophical issue, for our purposes we need not discuss it further.   It is enough for us to note that no matter what position we take on the question of freedom of the will, it would be admitted by all that our decisions and volitions often *do make a difference* to how things are.   And that is a very important fact, for it allows the opportunity for *values* and other moral considerations to play a role in determining how things are.

Let us imagine, to take a relevant example, that I am a male nearing his eighteenth birthday.   The law requires that I register for the draft.   Suppose I give the matter some thought.   I undertake a study of *how things are* to try to discover, among other things, the purposes of the law, the various possible consequences of registering or not registering, present American foreign and domestic policy, the effect of our military efforts on ourselves and the rest of the world, and so forth.   But in the end, I must decide *what I ought to do*— register or not register.   I think about what would be *good* or *bad* for me, for the nation, and for the world.   I think about what would be *right* and what would be *wrong* for me to do. I seek the opinions of others and ask advice of those I admire.   In the end, I must *decide what to do*.   Once I have done it, it is another fact, another case of *how things are*.   But how I decide will affect how things are, and this is true whether or not my decision is itself totally caused by factors that lie ultimately outside my control.   I can sometimes control my destiny, even if destiny ultimately may control me.

I can *choose* to register or not to register.   (A contribution of contemporary existentialist thought was to focus philosophical attention on the importance of the fact of choice.)   It is a terrible decision.   My whole life will be quite different as a consequence of how I decide.   If I could foresee the total consequences of each alternative, perhaps I would be in a better position to decide.   I would know better what I was deciding between.   But I can foresee very little.   Who can help me decide?   Many offer advice, even those who have faced the choice themselves and seen the consequences for them.   But who am I to listen to?   I do not know.   In terms of which principles am

I to decide—self-interest, the welfare of the nation, the welfare of mankind, respect for the wishes of my family and community? I cannot say. But this is clear—that I will have to decide, that no one can make the decision for me, that the consequences of my decision are not entirely predictable, that I will have to face those consequences and live with them, and that I will have to live with myself after I make my decision.

Of course I may not deliberate on this choice or even consciously make a decision. I may essentially let myself be pushed along. But even then, I have decided to acquiesce; I have still made my choice and I am responsible for it.

Suppose I do deliberate. There are two important elements here—my beliefs about *what is the case* and my desires, goals, and values concerning *what ought to be the case*. We have devoted some discussion in very general terms to the former element in our discussion of the nature of the physical world and its relation to the mind. It is now time we turned to the latter element—*values*.

What is a *value*? Let us begin by making the familiar philosophical distinction between values *as means* and values *as ends*. Getting money, for many, is a value, but very few would value getting money as an end in itself. Its value lies in what it helps us to achieve—the improvement of our own lot or the lot of others. When we inquire here about values, we are primarily interested in which things are *values as ends*— what is worthwhile not for its usefulness in achieving other things, but what is *worthwhile in and for itself*. For many, happiness, for example, is a value in this sense—it is worthwhile not for what it will bring us, but in and for itself.

We will also want to distinguish between such statements as "Most people value happiness," "Happiness is a value for most people," and "Most people believe (or hold) happiness to be a value" on the one hand, and "Happiness is a value" or "Happiness is valuable" on the other. The former group is made up of how-things-are statements—*descriptions* of people and the values they hold. The latter statements are how-things-ought-to-be statements—*evaluations* of happiness;

they claim that happiness is worthwhile, worthy of being valued, valuable, something people ought to value, something it would be correct for a person to value. It is in this latter respect that philosophers inquire into values. They want to investigate not what people in fact value (that is the job of anthropologists, sociologists, psychologists, economists, and political scientists), but what people ought to value.

Sometimes you will find people discussing whether "all values are relative." It is important to distinguish two separate issues here. (1) Are there any universal values? That is, are there any things that *every* culture, society, or ongoing group has valued? This is a how-things-are question about what people in fact value. The scientists concerned with this issues (in particular, anthropologists) do not agree, but one thing is clear, that many of the things valued in one society are not valued in all other societies. (2) Are there any things that all men *ought* to value? This question is one of whether any ought-to-be-valued-by-all-men statement can be held to be true.

It is quite clear that these two issues are separate ones. It *might* be the case that every ongoing group values continuing its existence; yet whether continuing its existence *ought* to be valued by every such group is quite another matter. The continued existence of a band of pirates and cutthroats might not be valuable even if the group itself values it. And it might be the case that no ongoing group endorses total pacifism, and yet it *might* be valuable that every group endorse total pacifism.

A value, then, as we are using that term, is something that is truly worthwhile and desirable *in itself* and *as an end* whether or not some proportion of a group in fact believes it to be a value. It is something that ought to exist whether in fact it does or does not and something that people ought to try to bring into existence whether in fact they do or do not.

Although we have been stressing the distinction between "is" and "ought," two points should be kept in mind. First, the distinction is not a totally sharp one; there is a borderline

area between the two.   There could be some debate as to
whether each of the following is an *is* (descriptive) or an
ought (evaluative) statement: "The Rolls Royce is a very
sound car," "She is a good daughter," "He is a master cellist,"
"You have obligated yourself to do it," and "I have the right
to a speedy trial."   But that goes for most distinctions.   There
is still a difference between red and yellow, even if there are
borderline cases.

Second, *ought* questions are not totally divorced from and
independent of *is* questions.   How things are in fact will have
considerable weight in leading us to determine what ought
to be.   In general, it will be the case that the more we know
about how things are, the wiser will be our decisions about
what ought to be.   In particular, the more we know about
human behavior and its relation to nature, the better are
our chances of finding answers to these basic questions of
ethics.

Let us take a particular example of the way *is* and *ought*
are related.   What people desire from moment to moment,
from day to day, is a question of how things are.   And from
the fact that something is desired, it does not follow that it
ought to be desired; that is to say, it does not follow that it is
worthy of desire or that it is desirable.   A person may mo-
mentarily desire to hurt someone, but he may admit that it
is not a worthy desire—that it is a desire he is ashamed of.
(Do you sometimes have unworthy desires?)   Even if the
person thinks it is worthy, he may be mistaken.   It is a fact
that the sadist desires to cause pain to another, but we cannot infer from that fact that his causing pain to another is
desirable.   Suppose the victim is a masochist, who desires to
be hurt.   Now things are more complicated.   Yet it still does
not follow that the pain is desirable; it follows only that it
is desired by both.   To make it follow that the pain is desirable, we need some further principle such as the principle
that it is desirable that human desires be satisfied (a puri-
tanical person might reject such a principle).   Of course, we
would need to clarify this principle a good deal to make it

stand up to rigorous scrutiny. We would want to consider whether it included *every* human desire, even those of children, the retarded, the mentally unwell, those drunk or on drugs, and so forth. And what if there are conflicts in desire either within the group or within the person himself? But if we succeeded in clarifying this principle, it might have considerable plausibility. A so-called utilitarian principle to the effect that an act is desirable if and only if it tends to contribute to the greatest happiness of the greatest number has been advocated by many, for example, John Stuart Mill in his book *Utilitarianism*.

What this discussion brings out is that in order to make the inference from an *is* statement to an *ought* statement, we need some sort of principle that says that such-and-such a state of affairs would be desirable or valuable or ought to be. Much of the discussion in moral philosophy today centers on the discussion of such principles—what they are, how they can be defended, and which, if any, are plausible. We will consider one such principle below.

16

The Meaning of Life

What do *you* personally hold to be truly valuable? What kind of a life do you want? Are there any general principles of conduct that you believe in? Do you think that these values hold for others as well? Do you think that there is anything it could be wrong for *anyone* to do?

Here are some things that have been variously proposed as the highest value or the greatest good: love, success, happiness, personal integrity, popularity, religious faith, wealth, pleasure, helping others, fame, understanding, self-development, power, the welfare of mankind (or some part of it, such as a particular race, religious group, nation, tribe, clan, community, or family), creative works, and freedom. Over the years each of these has had its defenders. Some may seem to you without value, and, of those you do believe to be genuine values, you may have difficulty ranking them. It is important to consider them in detail and try to rank them, but that would take us well beyond our purposes here.

When people speak of values and what they ought to value, they often raise a question to which we shall now turn, the question of *the meaning of life.* It is a common human experience to feel that sometimes life is not worth living. I am sure that many of you have had moments in your life when you felt terribly discouraged or frightened or when you found your situation extremely painful. In such a situation you might very well ask yourself such questions as: Why am I here? What is the point or purpose of all of this life? How does what is happening to me fit into some larger scheme of things? What is the significance of my life? What is the significance of life itself? What is the point of anything? Sometimes it is even put in a drastic form: Why should I go on living? What reason is there for me to continue to live from hour to hour and day to day? If you yourself have not actually felt this way, I'm sure that you recognize that there are very many people who, from time to time, have felt this way. What is the point of it all? What is it all about? Why go on? *What is the meaning of life?*

There are many circumstances in which this sort of feeling may come on you. Someone you love very much has just died or left you, and you are plunged into despair about it. Or you may have suffered some great disappointment—something you wanted very much and spent a long time trying to get is suddenly denied you. Or maybe you have just suffered some injury—maybe you're in great pain, or you've lost the use of a limb. Maybe you've become bedridden or no longer can perform some activity that was very important to you. Or else maybe you just look at the world and it seems to you suddenly that so many *other* people go through such horrible experiences or lead such miserable lives. Perhaps, being of a philosophical temper, you simply ask yourself what can be said for life as we know it. What is the point or purpose of it? Men over the centuries, as long as man has been a rational creature, have thought about this question and tried to answer it.

Socrates said the unexamined life is not worth living. This question of the meaning of life seems to be about the deepest and most profound question that someone who wishes to examine his life can raise.

One attempt to answer this question can be found in many religions. One of the main purposes of religions as we know them is to try to come to grips with this question—the meaning of life—and provide some sort of an answer for it. In general outline, most religions hold that there is some sort of supreme being, a deity, who has set up the world in a certain way, with certain purposes in mind, and that this deity has given each of us a particular role to play. We are all like members of His orchestra, and the purpose or point of each life is to live it in such a way as to make some kind of a contribution to the whole performance.

For the religious, the answer to the question, What is the meaning of life? consists in finding some role to play that will be a contribution to the total scheme or plan laid down by the deity. We may not know in detail what this scheme is or exactly how our life contributes to it, but we must go on whatever hints or clues religion can give us to tell how to live and give meaning to our lives.

But suppose one does not believe in the existence of a supreme being who has a plan. What kind of an answer can he give to the question, What is the meaning of life? He cannot appeal to some kind of an overall plan deliberately chosen by some supreme being in which each of us has a role to play and a contribution to make toward the whole scheme of things. From the theist's point of view, that is from the point of view of the person who believes in a supreme being with a plan, it looks as though the atheist's position is appallingly hopeless. To the theist, it looks as though for the atheist there is no purpose to life; life is just completely empty and without meaning; in the end we will all be dead and therefore our lives are just pointless exercises in futility; in the end we will be defeated by death and, as a result, our lives will have no significance. Is it true, as many theists (but not necessarily all) would contend, that they can give an answer to the question, What is the meaning of life? but the atheist cannot?

To answer this, we should first settle the question whether there is a supreme deity who has a plan. But it would not be fair for me to tell you and spoil the ending (of life) ! So let us leave this crucial question of God's existence open for you to pursue at another time. Let us concentrate on the simpler question, Is the atheist in a weaker position than the theist when the question of the meaning of life is raised? More precisely, Is it the case that the theist is able to believe that life does have a meaning whereas the atheist must hold that life has no meaning?

It is true that the atheist cannot give any answer to the question, What is the meaning of life? as the theist understands that question. Since the atheist rejects the notion of a supreme being, he rejects the notion of a supreme being with purposes and the notion of a supreme being who created the world and us in it to achieve those purposes. So if we ask the atheist *why we were put here,* he cannot give any answer.

However, it is clear why he cannot give any answer. He is at a disadvantage because *the very way in which the question is formulated* involves an assumption that he rejects. It looks as though it is a simple, single question, Why were we put here? but in fact the question cannot arise unless a prior question is answered, namely, Did anyone put us here for some purpose? That question must be answered in the affirmative before the further question, What is the purpose for which we were put here? can be answered. We have here a double-barreled question masquerading as a single question. In logic, this is sometimes called the fallacy of many questions. It comes up in the hackneyed legal example, "When did you stop beating your wife?" If I were asked that question, what could I say? Of course if I had been beating her, then I could give an answer to the question. I could say "last week," "never," or whatever the answer might be. But all of that presupposes that I had beat her in the past. Suppose I never had beat her; then I couldn't give an answer to the question,

"When did you stop beating your wife?" The fallacy of many questions comes up in many situations. "Is Jones still a Communist?" If he is not and had never been one, he cannot answer the question. How about: "Is the present king of France bald?" It, too, cannot be answered one way or the other if there is no present king of France.

So it is true that the atheist can give no answer to the question, Why were we put here? but it is no accident that he can't and no mark against his own theory. The very question as thus formulated presupposes a religious answer. If one rejects the presupposition, as the atheist does, then the question is illegitimate.

Suppose we reformulate the question so as to leave out this special theistic presupposition. Suppose we put the question as follows: What, if anything, makes life worth living? Now this question does admit of the possibility of a nontheistic answer. One might draw on some doctrines of Aristotle here. Aristotle held that the world is governed by a special kind of causation that he called teleological causation. Things undergo various sorts of changes toward the realization of certain goals or ends representing the fruition or coming into full realization of things. Thus the acorn is realized in the oak tree and the infant in the mature and rational man. One might say within the context of this view that what makes life worthwhile is the undergoing of a particular development that results in a certain end state or end product. This was made more individualistic by the Stoics, who held that each person has a niche in life—a station in life that was his realization and that gave point and significance to his life.

You may be familiar with the existentialist critique of such a view. Their position is summed up in the slogan "existence precedes essence." It means that none of us is from birth destined, fated, or doomed to any particular kind of development. We are free to develop as we choose, and we are free to choose not to develop. The simplest choice a man can make (although psychologically it is the most difficult) is to destroy himself. If we eventually become adult men of a particular sort, it is not because we were fated, predestined, or determined toward that end, but because we chose to achieve that end or let it happen. It seems to me that the existentialist is perfectly correct here. That is what distinguishes us from acorns. The acorn has no choice in developing into an oak. We do have choice, and our choices affect the sorts of men we become.

Many existentialists reject the theistic answer to the question of the meaning of life—the answer in terms of those divine purposes that are supposed to make life worthwhile. In rejecting that answer, many existentialists conclude that life is meaningless, pointless, and, to use a favorite existentialist word, "absurd." But this does not follow. From the premise that there are no ultimate purposes laid down for us, it does not follow that life has no meaning. It merely follows that life does not have the kind of meaning presupposed in the theistic formulation of the question.

Now let us look a little more closely at the religious answer to this question. In order for the religious answer to work at all, it is crucially necessary that the theist postulate some sort of a *benevolent* deity. This point is brought out very nicely in a passage by the British philosopher Bertrand Russell. Russell, at the time he wrote this, was himself *agnostic*—he believed that there is no way of telling whether or not there is a God, therefore, that the most reasonable position is complete suspension of either belief or disbelief. (There is a story that Russell told in his autobiography concerning the time he was sent off to jail in 1918 for urging young men to resist the draft. Russell said that when he arrived in prison, the jailer had to fill out some forms for him, and one of the questions was what Russell's religion was. Russell said he was an agnostic and the jailer, after asking him how to spell it, wrote it down, saying, "Well, there are many religions, but I suppose they all worship the same God." Russell said this remark kept him cheerful for a whole week.) In the following passage, Russell presented an imaginative account of the Creation:

To Dr. Faustus in his study Mephistopheles told the history of the Creation, saying:

"The endless praises of the choirs of angels had begun to grow wearisome; for, after all, did he not deserve their praise? Had he not given them endless joy? Would it not be more amuśing to obtain undeserved praise, to be worshipped by beings whom he tortured? He smiled inwardly, and resolved that the great drama should be performed.

"For countless ages the hot nebula whirled aimlessly through space. At length it began to take shape, the central mass threw off planets, the planets cooled, boiling seas and burning mountains heaved and tossed, from black masses of cloud hot sheets of rain deluged the barely solid crust. And now the first germ of life grew in the depths of the ocean, and developed rapidly in the fructifying warmth into vast forest trees, huge ferns springing from the damp mould, sea monsters breeding, fighting, devouring, and passing away. And from the monsters, as the play unfolded itself, Man was born, with the power of thought, the knowledge of good and evil, and the cruel thirst for worship. And Man saw that all is struggling to snatch, at any cost, a few brief moments of life before Death's inexorable decree. And Man said: 'There is a hidden purpose, could we but fathom it, and the purpose is good; for we must reverence something, and in the visible world there is nothing worthy of reverence.' And Man stood aside from the struggle, resolving that God intended harmony to come out of chaos by human efforts. And when he followed the instincts which God had transmitted to him from his ancestry of beasts of prey, he called it Sin, and asked God to forgive him. But he doubted whether he could be justly forgiven, until he invented a divine Plan by which God's wrath was to have been appeased. And seeing the present was bad, he made it yet worse, that thereby the future might be better. And he gave God thanks for the strength that enabled him to forgo even the joys that were possible. And God smiled; and when he saw that Man had become perfect in renunciation and worship, he sent another sun through the sky, which crashed into Man's sun; and all returned again to nebula.

" 'Yes,' he murmured, 'it was a good play; I will have it performed again.' " [1]

---

[1] Bertrand Russell, "A Free Man's Worship," *Mysticism and Logic* (London: George Allen & Unwin, Ltd., 1917), pp. 46–47.

Let us suppose that Russell's imaginative account is true and that things really happened that way. Would one be inclined to say that life does in fact have a meaning, point, or significance, that we do now have a rational answer to the question, What is the meaning of life? I think we would agree that if Russell's fantasy accurately describes how things were, it would not be the case that life has significance or meaning. We would all of us be victims of a cruel and sadistic deception, and our lives would be meaningless and not, in fact, worth living.

What we need then, on the theistic account, is a *benevolent* deity—a being who wishes well for us and has our best interests at heart. It is not necessary that the whole scheme of things be directed in our favor; but God's ultimate purpose must be one that we believe to be worthwhile, and our role in it must be to contribute to this worthwhile end. And that means we have to ask ourselves, even if we do believe in God, what we would consider a worthwhile end to be. Russell's example shows that we would not consider it a worthwhile end simply to contribute to the gratification and amusement of some sadistic deity. So, even the theist must ask himself what would be a worthwhile end—one that would give meaning and value to life.

Let us consider, just as a sample, an answer that would satisfy some theists (although it should be pointed out that many theists would find other answers more truly in the spirit of religion). Some theists would hold that the worthwhile end that would give life importance and significance would be some sort of an *afterlife* of eternal bliss and happiness. They would hold that if such an eternally happy life is in store for us, then life is indeed worth living and does have point and significance. This life would be a means to a valuable and significant end.

Let us see what is going on here. Why would this sort of a religious answer satisfy many people? Because they believe that a happy life is in itself *valuable and worthwhile,* so much so that certain sacrifices would be justified if they led to such a life. Now where does the belief in God come in here? Well, it is the existence of God that guarantees that we will achieve such an end.   Or rather it makes it *more likely* that we will achieve such an end, since in most religions we are not *guaranteed* eternal happiness.   It is not that the existence of God makes happiness worthwhile; it is simply that *He makes it attainable.*   However, it should be pointed out here that the atheist can also grasp the desirability of happiness and agree that it would make life worthwhile.   So if we are atheists but believe that human happiness is attainable by human effort and that pain and suffering are worthwhile sacrifices if they bring about great happiness, then we too, as atheists, may hold that life is worthwhile insofar as it does bring happiness.

There are those pessimists, like Schopenhauer, who hold that happiness is simply not attainable for mankind.   This, of course, is a factual matter.   It is a suggestion of many forms of theism that if life as we know it is all there is, then there is not enough happiness in life to make it worth living.   Is this claim true?   I suppose it is true that many lives have not contained enough happiness to make them worth living, but I would doubt very much that this is true of all lives, or even of most.   Of course, in comparison with heaven as many conceive it, this life probably is not worth living.   This life falls so far short of eternal happiness as to be almost worthless *in comparison,* but why should one think that just because this life falls short of eternal happiness it is so miserable as to be not worth living?

It is my own view that for most of us there is a real opportunity and good chance for happiness.   I believe that for most of us the amount of happiness attainable does make life worth living, but I am willing to admit that this is a personal judgment and one with which many would not agree.

So far we have concentrated on happiness because we were taking as our starting point the view that what makes life worthwhile is the prospect of eternal happiness.   But this, of course, is only one of a number of possible religious views.   There are those religious thinkers who have held that what makes life worthwhile is not the happiness in store for us, but what a person makes of his life here; many atheists would agree. Mill said that it is better to be Socrates dissatisfied than a fool satisfied. I am sure that there are many who find the meaning and value of life not in a blissful state of happiness, but in living for some particular cause. They feel that they wish to dedicate their life to enriching the lives of others, creating beautiful things, or contributing to the creation of something that will endure beyond their own lifetime. These may very well be entirely suitable goals, and each may be adopted by a person whether he is a theist or an atheist.

Let us now return to the question whether the theist has an advantage over the atheist concerning the question of the meaning of life. We have seen that the usual way of putting the question involves the fallacy of many questions. The properly neutral way of putting the question is to ask: What, if anything, gives life value and makes it worth living? When the question is thus put, it is clear that the atheist is in no weaker a position than the theist. Each will offer certain values, for example, happiness; they may well offer the *very same values.*

Does the theist have this advantage: his faith that in the end God will make sure that our ends are achieved? As has been noted already, most theists would not say that anything is guaranteed. But whatever degree of faith the theist has in the outcome of things, cannot the atheist have a corresponding faith that all will turn out well? It would seem that optimism is not to be allowed to the theist but denied to the atheist. Of course, some theists look forward to an *eternity* of well-being, whereas the atheist usually cannot. But a value does not cease to be a value because it only lasts a finite time. If it is worthwhile, then it is worthwhile for as long as it exists, even if it does not exist forever.

Russell's imaginary Creation shows that in the end each of us must judge for himself what has value. We would not accept as meaningful and worthwhile the kind of life depicted in his fantasy. Each must decide for himself. This means that the meaning or purpose of one's life is something that *one takes on* rather than something that is predestined for one's life. It is something that one adopts for oneself rather than something that is dictated to one. The meaning or purpose of life is a program that one adopts or accepts for oneself. You are familiar, perhaps, with the use of the word "program" that applies to computers. A computer is idle or useless until it is given a program; here is one most important way in which man is different. We are *self-programing;* we have the power and the capacity to adopt a program for our own lives. We can program ourselves, and in doing so, we may be able to live out a life that strikes us as being a meaningful and significant life.

Just as a theist may try to lend support to his value choices by claiming that God endorses those values ("God is on our side"), so an atheist may try to gain support for his values by claiming that nature or history is on his side. Thus, the social Darwinist may appeal to evolutionary theory to support his valuing of aggressive acquisition and competitive victory. The Marxist may appeal to the alleged historical inevitability of the classless society to justify his efforts against capitalism. There is that deep need that some of us have to see our efforts as part of some underlying pattern "dictated" if not by God then by the laws of nature or the laws of history. But the point made against theism is relevant here. We can judge that nature is evil and should be thwarted or that the direction of history ought to be changed. It is up to us to decide how things ought to be, what values to endorse, and what is worthwhile in life.

What if, in terms of the values one has endorsed, the quality of one's life is, after all, worthless? What if one has sought happiness and failed? What if one has not found a program to adopt that will give him satisfaction and make his life meaningful? Why should one go on living in such a case? I can think of three things to say in answer to such a question. First, very few lives need be utterly worthless. There is always some cause or some program that can be adopted that will advance some worthwhile end. Of course, we may not be able to tell at the time; only the future can decide whether good will come of our efforts, but until we have tried, we cannot tell. We always run the risk of having lived in vain, of having lived a life that did, in fact, turn out to be worthless. This might come about if we had devoted our whole life to some cause and the cause failed or we came to see that the cause itself was not good. But one cannot tell what the outcome will be until one has tried as far as one can.

Second, things often improve; it may well be that our life at present is worthless; but life is full of surprises and changes, and there is always the possibility that what has been up until now a worthless life will be presented with the possibility of taking on significance and meaning. Third, it does seem to me that there may be cases in which one can be fairly sure that no worthwhile cause can be adopted, that no values can be achieved. Some people afflicted with terminal illnesses may be of this sort, living lives filled with pain, where the illness has progressed so far that there is no longer any hope of improvement. Here there may well be absolutely no point in the continuance of life, no value to be gained from postponing death. In such cases, I am inclined to think that the individual concerned, if he wishes, should be allowed to terminate his life. What do *you* think? Are there other cases for which you think suicide or euthanasia (mercy killing) might be justified?

17

Values and Consciousness

Just as we saw earlier that the studies of epistemology and metaphysics are interconnected—procedures and results in one bear on procedures and results in the other—so both studies are related to ethics. I wish to indicate in this last section a few cases of important interrelations.

We have just seen, in the preceding section an example of the relation of ethics to metaphysics and epistemology. The question of whether there is a God is a *metaphysical* question and the question of whether we can have any knowledge of such a being is an *epistemological* question. Yet as we have seen both bear very importantly on questions concerning values and meaning in life.

If we consider the various things that have been proposed as values (see page 101), we will notice that most if not all of them involve a mental component. Both loving and being loved involve *awareness*. Many people strive for success, but part of being a success is *being aware of it*. Happiness is in part, at least, a state of mind. And so on for the large majority of values that have been proposed. It has been debated by philosophers whether *every* true value necessarily has a component involving consciousness. Could there, for example, be any values or anything valuable in a world forever empty of conscious beings? Most philosophers today, I would guess, would say No to that question.

Some philosophers have gone so far as to say that values reside totally and completely in certain states of mind. Thus, for example, it has been held by some that pleasurable mental states alone are intrinsically valuable—worthwhile in themselves. Others, while agreeing that states of mind are necessary components, would hold that the state of mind is not sufficient for value; we must also take into account the circumstances. They would cite a case such as the pleasure of a sadist enjoying another's torture as a case in which the value of the pleasurable mental state is reduced to zero by the circumstances in which it occurs. It might be replied that the pleasure of the sadist is still good in itself even if the pain of the victim is bad. After all, at least one of them is happy, and that is better than both of them being miserable. If torture must occur, is it not better that the torturer enjoy his work than that it make him unhappy?

A more realistic case is as follows. Most would agree that the conscious state of aesthetic enjoyment is a value. Now it is the case that certain drugs can sometimes make things without any aesthetic merit at all seem very beautiful. Is such aesthetic enjoyment valuable? Consider a drug that induces a state of great happiness no matter what the circumstances. Is such a state valuable? Is the semicomatose state of bliss of the opium smoker valuable in itself? These questions are too important to be dismissed with a brief comment; I will leave them to the reader (and to the author) for further thought.

Let us now consider another respect in which questions of ethics are related to questions of epistemology and metaphysics. I want to use as an example a moral judgment that would gain the assent of most readers of this book. I have chosen the following: *It is intrinsically wrong to inflict great pain on another against his will just for the fun of it.* To make this judgment appeal to as many as possible, I specify that the pain must be *great* (since some might believe that there is nothing wrong if the pain is minor and the fun enormous, perhaps in certain practical jokes or in teasing), that it must be *against his will* (since some might believe that inflicting pain on a masochist, who welcomes it, is not wrong), and that it must be *just for the fun of it* (since there may well be cases in which it is not wrong to inflict great pain on another against his will; there may be very good reasons to do so—it may be necessary in order to save his life). Finally, I am thinking of an act that is *intrinsically* wrong, that is, wrong in itself and not wrong because of any further consequences of the act. If the judgment is understood with these points in mind, I would guess that the vast majority of readers would accept the judgment as true.

Another matter, and a terribly difficult matter, is *how* we know the judgment is true. It is so simple and basic a judgment that it is unlikely that it could be deduced from some other judgment or judgments. Even if it could be so deduced, that would just leave us with exactly the same problem: How do we know the judgment or judgments from which it is deduced? The theist might say we know it to be true because God tells us it is true. But how do we know God really tells us it is true? And, more important, so what? Suppose some supernatural being told us it was all right to inflict great pain for the fun of it? We would say that such a being was evil! In other words, we already know the judgment to be true and would not call a supernatural being "God" unless that being also assented to the judgment.

Perhaps the best that can be said for the judgment is that it is *self-evident*. If this means, however, that *anyone* who considered it would assent to it, then it must be admitted that it might well *not* be self-evident to *everyone*. There are people, sadists, for example, who do inflict pain for the fun of it. Although some of them might admit it is wrong of them to do so, others might see nothing wrong in it, and we might not be able to succeed in persuading them that there is anything wrong in it. Suppose we said, "How would you like us to do it to you?" The sadist might admit that *he* would not like that at all, but he might still claim that there was nothing *wrong* in it. (I might not like you to beat me at tennis, but I could not say it would be *wrong* of you to beat me at tennis.) So we cannot say that such a judgment would seem self-evidently true to everyone. Now the sadist is usually thought of as suffering from an illness, a behavior disorder; he is a psychopath. So the best we can say, and perhaps not even this is true, is that the judgment is self-evident to any *normal* person. But now we would still need a definition of "normal" that does not involve begging the question by calling someone abnormal just because he does not find such judgments self-evidently true. And that is not easy to provide.

The above considerations concern the question *how we know* the judgment that it is wrong to inflict pain for the fun of it. From the fact that it is very difficult to say how we know, it does not follow that we do not know. It seems to me that we do know this judgment to be true, even if we cannot say how we know it. Imagine someone inflicting considerable pain on a child just for the fun of it. Isn't it so clear and obvious, can't you just *see* that it is wrong? I think we do indeed have here a moral judgment that would gain the assent of most readers despite the epistemological difficulties involved.

Now we shall consider the relevance of such a judgment to metaphysics. Earlier we considered some theories concerning the nature of such mental events as the feeling of pain. One such theory was labeled materialism (see section 12)—the view that all events in nature are physical (atoms and the void) and that so-called mental events are therefore nothing but purely physical occurrences. According to the view called behaviorism, they are items of physical behavior or dispositions toward such items of behavior. According to the identity theory, they are brain events—the firings of neural cells, waves of electrical energy, or the like.

Now let us consider our moral judgment concerning pain in the light of these materialistic theories. For the behaviorist, a feeling of pain would be the exhibiting, under the appropriate circumstances, of pain-behavior: groans, grimaces, paleness of face, clenching of the teeth, writhings, and so forth. Our moral judgment would come to this: It is intrinsically wrong to induce in another person groans, grimaces, and so forth, just for the fun of it. But is the judgment true under the behavioristic interpretation? I, for one, cannot see that it is. What is wrong about inducing that sort of behavior in another? Of course, one might hold that it is wrong to induce *any* sort of behavior in another against his will just for the fun of it. But that would be a different principle, although one that would also command the assent of most of us. But the principle we are concerned with holds that it is particularly wrong to induce groans, grimaces, and so forth. And I do not believe that this is the case. To see this, consider giving our victim curare prior to torture. A sufficient dose of curare leaves a person fully conscious and able to feel everything but, temporarily, completely paralyzed and unable to respond behaviorally. On the behavioristic account, we can erase the wrongness of the act by administering curare before tightening the thumb screws or turning on the electricity. If what is intrinsically wrong in eliciting that behavior, then the use of curare would make everything all right. But, of course, it does not. For it is not the dispositions to behavior that are intrinsically undesirable. If that is all there is to pain, our moral judgment would not be true. If our judgment is true, there must be more to pain than the behavior to which we are disposed. If behaviorism is true, our moral judgment loses its validity. Our moral principle and behaviorism cannot both be true (though they could both be false). Which are we to give up?

Even if we did not have prior arguments against behaviorism

(see pp. 75–76) , I believe we would accept the moral principle and reject behaviorism if forced to choose between the two. The moral principle seems intuitively quite certain and undeniable, whereas behaviorism has a considerably lower degree of likelihood. If forced to choose, it is reasonable to pick the more likely one.

If one is inclined toward the view that we earlier labeled fallibilism, then there is a related reason for rejecting behaviorism. Because the considerations in support of behaviorism are more complex, there are more chances of going wrong in thinking about the matter. If the mere possibility of mistakes of various sorts decreases the warrant (see page 26) , then behaviorism cannot have the degree of likelihood that the moral principle has.

Do similar considerations apply to the identity theory? It would seem so, but it is not as clear a matter in this case. According to the identity theory, our moral principle comes to this: It is intrinsically wrong to stimulate certain parts of a man's brain. Put that way, the principle is certainly no longer obvious or self-evident. It is even doubtful whether it is true. Many of those who accept the original principle as true would reject this principle as false.

But now the identity theorist would claim that it is because we are *ignorant* of the identity that we would accept the original principle yet reject the identity version of it. After all, he would argue, if infliction of pain is wrong, and pain is identical with stimulation of a particular part of the brain, then that stimulation is wrong.

One might grant the identity theorist this logical point but still question his line of reasoning. Does he not beg the question? The logical point is relevant on the assumption that we already know the identity. But we are trying to decide whether there is an identity of brain states and mental states. We can appeal to the fact that pain has a moral undesirability whereas the corresponding brain state does not have this moral undesirability. This fact, if it is a fact, would show that pain and the brain state are not identical. And when we add this argument against the identity theory to the others we considered earlier, we have even more reason to reject it.

These matters, as well as many others in this introduction to philosophy, are still actively debated by contemporary philosophers. This fact should not be surprising to us, for the problems we have discussed in this book are among the most difficult ever encountered by man, and they have been found deeply puzzling by the greatest intellects our species has produced. Yet progress has been made. The greatest of the philosophers of the past would find things to learn in what is philosophical common knowledge today, just as we can still learn from reading them.

This has been an introduction in two respects. First, there is hardly a sentence in it that could not be questioned, and a careful reader would have found himself questioning many. Second, we have considered only a small sample of the issues that could be raised under the headings of metaphysics, epistemology, and ethics. Let us hope you have found this discussion sufficiently challenging to lead you to pursue these matters further. There is no better way of closing than with the words Spinoza used to close his great metaphysical treatise the *Ethics:*

> If the way . . . seems very difficult, it can nevertheless be found. It must indeed be difficult since it is so seldom discovered; for if salvation lay ready to hand and could be discovered without great labor, how could it be possible that it should be neglected almost by everybody? But all noble things are as difficult as they are rare.

FURTHER READINGS

For additional readings in philosophy, one can take a number of different paths. An excellent companion to this book is John Hospers' *Readings in Introductory Philosophical Analysis* (Englewood Cliffs, N.J.: Prentice-Hall, 1968), containing selections from historical and contemporary sources. The issues I discuss concerning the possibility of knowledge [SECTIONS 1–6] are discussed in Parts One to Three of his book; the problem of perception [SECTIONS 7–10] in his Part Five; the problem of free will [SECTION 15] in his Part Four; the existence of God [SECTION 16] in his Part Six; and problems of ethics [SECTIONS 15–17] in his Part Eight. John Hospers' *An Introduction to Philosophical Analysis*, 2nd ed. (Englewood Cliffs, N.J.: Prentice-Hall, 1967), is a systematic introductory text that provides a thorough examination of these and other contemporary issues.

For further readings on the topics in this book, the following may be of interest (arranged within each section in order of increasing difficulty):

KNOWLEDGE AND PERCEPTION [SECTIONS 1–10]

Scheffler, Israel. *Conditions of Knowledge.* Glenview, Ill.: Scott, Foresman and Co., 1965.
Ayer, A. J. *The Foundations of Empirical Knowledge.* London: Macmillan and Co., Ltd., 1964.

122   FURTHER READINGS

Austin, J. L. *Sense and Sensibilia.* New York: Oxford University Press, 1964.
Malcolm, Norman. *Knowledge and Certainty.* Englewood Cliffs, N.J.: Prentice-Hall, 1963.
Chisholm, Roderick M. *Theory of Knowledge.* Englewood Cliffs, N.J.: Prentice-Hall, 1966.

Anthologies:

Griffiths, A. Phillips. *Knowledge and Belief.* London: Oxford University Press, 1967.
Ammerman, Robert R., and Marcus G. Singer. *Belief, Knowledge and Truth.* New York: Scribner, 1970.
Swartz, Robert J. *Perceiving, Sensing, and Knowing.* New York: Doubleday, 1965.

MIND AND BODY [SECTIONS 11–14]

Shaffer, Jerome A. *Philosophy of Mind.* Englewood Cliffs, N.J.: Prentice-Hall, 1968.
Ryle, Gilbert. *The Concept of Mind.* New York: Barnes & Noble, 1949.
Wisdom, John. *Other Minds.* Oxford: Blackwell, 1952.

Anthologies:

Chappell, V. C. *The Philosophy of Mind.* Englewood Cliffs, N.J.: Prentice-Hall, 1962.
Morick, Harold. *Introduction to the Philosophy of Mind.* Glenview, Ill.: Scott, Foresman and Co., 1970.
Flew, Antony. *Body, Mind, and Death.* New York: Macmillan, 1964.

VALUES [SECTIONS 15–17]

Frankena, William K. *Ethics.* Englewood Cliffs, N.J.: Prentice-Hall, 1963.
Hospers, John. *Human Conduct.* New York: Harcourt, Brace & Jovanovich, 1961.
Nowell-Smith, P. H. *Ethics.* London: Penguin Books, Ltd., 1954.

Hare, R. M. *The Language of Morals.* Oxford: The Clarendon Press, 1952.

Hare, R. M. *Freedom and Reason.* Oxford: The Clarendon Press, 1963.

Anthologies:

Melden, A. I. *Ethical Theories.* 2nd ed. Englewood Cliffs, N.J.: Prentice-Hall, 1955.

Brandt, R. B. *Value and Obligation.* New York: Harcourt, Brace & Jovanovich, 1961.

Olafson, Frederick. *Justice and Social Policy.* Englewood Cliffs, N.J.: Prentice-Hall, 1961.

Feinberg, Joel. *Moral Concepts.* Oxford: Oxford University Press, 1969.

The reader may wish to turn to the writings of some of the great historical figures who have made important contributions to these problems. The following are recommended:

Edman, Irwin (ed.). *The Philosophy of Plato.* New York: Random House. 1928.

Descartes, Rene. *Meditations.* New York: The Liberal Arts Press, 1951.

Berkeley, George (ed.). *Three Dialogues between Hylas and Philonous.* New York: The Liberal Arts Press, 1954.

Hendel, Charles W., Jr. *Hume: Selections.* New York: Scribner, 1927.

INDEX

ABOUT THE AUTHOR

JEROME A. SHAFFER is a professor of philosophy at the University of Connecticut, having for-
merly taught at Swarthmore. He received his B.A.
from Cornell and his Ph.D. from Princeton in 1952.
During 1963 he was a Fellow at the Center for Advanced Study in the Behavioral Sciences in Stanford, and he has been executive secretary of the
Council for Philosophical Studies since 1965. Currently concentrating his studies on epistemology,
metaphysics, and the philosophy of mind, Professor
Shaffer is the author of *Philosophy of Mind*
(1968), and contributes frequently to several philosophical journals.